Embodied Grace
Trusting Yourself, Healing Deeply, Expanding Fully
Stacey Webb

Stacey Webb

Cover design by Heidi Glasson
Interior design by Stacey Webb
Interior images by Heidi Glasson

ISBN: (Paperback) 978-0-6458119-4-0
ISBN: (Ebook) 978-0-6458119-5-7

To Vanessa, Rhiannon, Ashton, and Adeline.

My inspiration, my heart, my purpose. You are the reason I continue to seek growth, compassion, and grace. Mummy loves you very much.

And to my younger self,

You are loved, you are enough, and you have always been worthy of grace.

Acknowledgements of Country

I honour the Dharug and Gundungurra peoples of the Ngurra Nation whose land cradled the writing of *Embodied Grace: Trusting Yourself, Healing Deeply, Expanding Fully.* This land has been cared for and lived on by generations before us. Every tree, stone, and blade of grass carries their wisdom.

I bow to the earth beneath my feet, to the waters that flow through this country, and to the vast skies above. All hold stories and memories older than we can imagine. May I walk gently here with respect and gratitude.

I acknowledge the Elders, past and present, who hold the spirit of this land alive with their care, their teachings, and their deep connection.

I also honour the traditional Tamil lands in India, where this work grew and deepened. These ancient lands, alive with spirit and wisdom offered a sacred space for this book to unfold. Their teachings of care, compassion, and connection continue to light the way.

With deep respect and gratitude, I hold these places and peoples in my heart. May the spirit of this work be touched by their grounding presence, and may their wisdom flow through these pages.

Acknowledgment of my Teachers and Mentors

I honour the teachers, mentors, and sacred lineages who have walked beside me, both seen and unseen, whispering wisdom into the marrow of my becoming.

Their presence has gently stretched me beyond my comfort, inviting me to shed old skins, soften into truth, and trust the unfolding of my soul's path.

Through their tender challenge and fierce compassion, I have learned to meet myself with grace. They held the mirror when I couldn't see, reminding me of the strength that lived beneath my doubt, and guided me home to my own inner knowing.

Each carries a thread in the sacred web that supports this work, from ancient keepers of wisdom to present-day visionaries. Their imprint hums through every word, every breath, every offering held here.

May their teachings ripple outward, touching those who find their way to these pages. And may this work be an offering of reverence, for the journey, for the teachers, and for the unshakable wisdom that lives within us all.

To learn more about the teachers who have shaped this path, please refer to the resource section.

Author Note

This book is part memoir, and all of the events are true to the best of the author's memory. To protect the privacy of certain individuals, some names and identifying details have been altered.

It is important to note that the information, practices, and tools shared in this book are based on my experiences and research as a somatic practitioner and intuitive somatic mentor. This book is not intended as professional advice or a substitute for personal or medical services. The author assumes no responsibility for any actions taken based on the content of this book. Readers are encouraged to consult with a healthcare professional before engaging in any of the practices described within.

Contents

Supporting Your Exploration

To support your journey of Embodied Grace, I have created free resources that include Embodied Insights journaling prompts and guided practice recordings mentioned throughout the book.

Access them at https://www.staceywebb.com.au/embodiedgraceresources

Embodied Grace Resources QR

Foreward

Stacey Webb is a woman seemingly without limits. She is probably laughing as she reads this, mentally checking off all of her self-assessed limits! So what I really mean to say is that Stacey lives graciously beyond any stories, ideas, self-perceptions, demands, or excuses. I have never met anyone like Stacey in this regard, and I am grateful every day that she found the Institute for Intuitive Intelligence's work, so that I have the privilege of knowing her.

Stacey blows me away in the best possible way every time we are together. With four children, a demanding profession as a Police Detective, and a wife to another emergency services professional who works 24-hour shifts and is regularly away from the family home for extended periods of time, Stacey has every reason to leave it at that!

But leave it at that; she has not. For years, Stacey has also, in addition to all of the above, been on a path of self-realisation, beginning with training as a Somatic Practitioner to better understand her own nervous system responses and those of her colleagues. She has trained in Emotional Freedom Technique and breathwork. When she found the Institute and began the journey to become an Intuitive Intelligence® Trainer, she was already writing her first book, *The Intuitive Detective*. She went on to qualify as an Intuition Teacher with the Institute, and somewhere in there, wrote her second book, *Foundations of Tapping*.

The Intuitive Detective was released in 2022 and has since won many awards. It is not a surprise. Stacey offered us all a glimpse into a world that most of us will never see from the inside. She did this through an extraordinary lens - that of intuition and how her innate intuition supported her in her policing work.

It is a captivating book, deeply personal and extraordinarily insightful. *An intuitive detective?* So much of this book challenged my ideas of the police force and the work of first responders. It also gave me a deep appreciation for Stacey's courage, grace and wisdom. Stacey brought two seemingly disparate worlds together with respect and reverence for both. She showed me, and undoubtedly many others, that these two worlds can and should be united to support all of us better. It was a bold leap, a public outing of Stacey's many parts, and I bow to her willingness to be a leader in this way. I have no doubt there was fear in publicly declaring her intuitive self to her professional world, but she did it anyway.

The term "thought leader" gets thrown around a lot. Forbes describes a thought leader as '*...having a unique point of view and consistently living it. You must demonstrate strength and discipline in all your actions. You must have clarity about your purpose.*'*

I can think of no better description of Stacey and the work she offers the world. Stacey is a thought leader because she embodies what she offers others. She is the demonstration, not through a highly curated public image, but in her authentic expression, her clarity, her drive, her no-excuses mentality.

Stacey is congruent between her faith and her actions, and she shows up, not because it is easy or because she has time to spare (she does not), but because she knows the power of what she offers others. She knows, because she has humbly sat at the feet of her own teachings and allowed them to transform her. Stacey positively changed my perspective on the kind of person I could serve. It felt like a huge honour to be Stacey's spiritual teacher. Here was a woman willing to risk the safety of her well-respected professional identity to invite us all to ask, 'What else is possible?'

In the time I have had the privilege of knowing Stacey, she has grown more and more into her self-assurance, her confidence, and her authentic joy. She is embodied grace. Not because life is easy. But because she made the choice, and humbly followed it through. There is a well-worn adage: *if you want something done, give it to a busy woman.*

Stacey gets it done. Whatever she sets her mind to. In a few short months from when the idea for *Embodied Grace* formed on our retreat in India, she had a first draft. Now, just over a year later, she is ready to share her new book with the world. I am humbled. I am awed and constantly inspired.

Embodied Grace reflects the maturing of Stacey's identity as a bridge between worlds. If *The Intuitive Detective* was a bold leap into the unknown that changed so many lives, *Embodied Grace* is a homecoming. The self-assurance I have witnessed over the last few years blooms forth from these pages. Her writerly voice has matured as she has honed her craft, and, deeper than that, given herself permission to embody all that she is publicly. It is a book that creates deep somatic safety for the reader, because that is what Stacey has created for herself.

This book is exactly what we all need: a warm embrace that whispers, *all parts of you are welcome.* Stacey brings her gift for storytelling to her new book, and it is a pleasure to read the next chapter in her story, which began in *The Intuitive Detective.* It is a profound resource, full of tools and processes shared with the richness and depth of someone who has practised them all herself, again and again. Stacey is not shouting at us from the mountaintop. She is in the trenches beside us, shoulder to shoulder, inviting us to remember that grace is here and now.

I describe grace as what God feels like. In this book, Stacey shows us the path to that God-realisation in the day-to-day, the mundane, the life-changing, the heartbreaking, and the sublime. She offers us a way to be in grace, not as some far-off ideal, but just as we are right now.

Please take your time with this book. Let it alter you. Stacey has generously offered us a direct path to embody grace in our own lives, if we are willing not just to consume the words but to sink into the practices and connect to the energy of the author, so seamlessly woven into every word. To journey with this book feels like having Stacey right by your side, every step of the way. And that is a blessing not to be squandered.

Dr Ricci-Jane Adams
Principal of the Institute for Intuitive Intelligence®
January 2026

**https://www.forbes.com/councils/forbesagencycouncil/2023/04/19/what-it-really-means-and-takes-to-become-a-thought-leader/*

A Letter from My Heart

Hello beautiful soul,

Welcome. I'm so glad you found your way here.

You've entered a space where there's no need to perform, prove, or be perfect. Just you, as you are, is more than enough here. This book was born from my healing, a journey that began long before I became a mother and continues still, as I learn to return to myself again and again.

From my earliest memories, I tied my sense of worth to how well I met others' expectations. As a child, I sought praise and approval like lifelines, shaping myself to fit the needs of those around me. I became a master of masks, hiding the parts of me that felt messy or unlovable, even from my eyes.

Each time I denied my feelings, desires, or truths, I unknowingly said to myself, *Who I am is not enough.* By my teenage years, this belief had sunk deep into my bones. When I looked in the mirror, I didn't see someone worthy of love. I saw someone whose value depended on being enough: pretty enough, smart enough, nice enough. Always enough in someone else's eyes.

It wasn't just about appearances or achievements. If I let someone down, even in the smallest way, I would berate myself for days. A single misstep could unravel my sense of self-worth. I lived in a cycle of chasing external validation while feeling unworthy of my love and care.

That pattern followed me as I got older, shaping my relationships and my inner world. On days when I felt seen or validated, I believed I was worthy of living fully, of showing up, engaging, and taking up space. But on the days I didn't, the inner critic took over. I questioned everything about myself. I turned to coping mechanisms of binge eating and binge drinking to numb the ache of disconnection. But each time I numbed, the shame deepened, leaving me more disconnected from both my body and soul.

It was while working as a detective, surrounded by people experiencing trauma, that I first explored the world of healing. I listened to victims recount unimaginable pain, accompanied them to identify loved ones at the morgue, and witnessed their courage in court. The more I supported others, the more I realised I had never truly held space for my fears, emotions, and needs.

Recognising this, I sought support from a somatic practitioner. Through that work, I learnt how trauma had lodged in my body and what my nervous system truly needed. Inspired, I trained—both before and during motherhood—as a Somatic Practitioner, Intuitive Intelligence Teacher, and Spiritual Director. These experiences, both lived and studied, shaped my identity as an Intuitive Somatic Mentor, guided by both personal experience and formal learning.

Becoming a mother was the next profound chapter. I was filled with joy, anticipation, and a sense of wonder at the life growing within me. At the same time, I was confronted by how deeply my old patterns were ingrained. My eldest, Vanessa, and Rhiannon, were born within a few years of each other, and those early years were a blur of exhaustion, love, and discovery. Later, twins Ashton and Adeline were born, and when Ashton was diagnosed with ADHD and Autism at four, I was reminded to slow down, listen differently, and meet each child and myself with greater presence.

Motherhood became a mirror, revealing what needed to change and inviting me to embody grace, presence, and care throughout my life. I realised I could no longer live by old patterns of perfectionism, self-sabotage, and control and had to create a new path grounded in wholeness, compassion, and truth.

In 2024, I answered a soul-deep calling and embarked on a sacred pilgrimage to an area in the South East of India near Pondicherry (Pudicherry), as part of my studies to become a Spiritual Director. One grounded in a non-denominational, heart-centred approach that honours the Divine in all forms. The path of the Spiritual Director in the program I studied isn't tied to any one tradition, but invites a deep listening to spirit, intuition, and the sacred wisdom that lives within and around us.

On the first evening in India, I stood under a luminous sky. The stars pierced the clear night air, and there, glowing softly above me, was a moon unlike any I had seen before. A slender waxing crescent rested on the right side, delicate and bright. Within it, faint yet unmistakable, was the full circle of the moon's outline. It was as if the moon was revealing both its current phase and its fullness all at once. A message whispered through the night sky, "Even when only part of you is visible to the world, your wholeness remains complete, radiant, and held." The sight captivated me, as though it had been placed in the heavens just for me.

Later that evening, when I stepped into the *shala* 'place' for our first gathering, I was met by a sacred hush. The air held the soft scent of sandalwood and rose incense. The temperature in the room was just right, holding me in a gentle, welcoming embrace. Candlelight flickered gently along the walls, casting a golden glow.

At the front of the *shala* stood an altar, adorned with fresh marigolds, flickering oil lamps, statues of deities, and offerings of fruit and flowers. It felt grounding and sacred.

In the middle of the *shala* was a mandala made of petals, crystals, and leaves carefully arranged. Around it were small offerings: bowls of water, sacred herbs, and handwritten intentions placed beneath smooth stones. Everything in the space felt intentional, tender, and alive.

Yoga mats and cushions were arranged in a circle around the centre. Some of my sisters sat in silence, while others had their eyes closed, hands resting over their hearts. A soft chant played, soothing and steady, like a heartbeat.

As we came into the evening's practice, our teacher invited us to reflect on our *sankalpa*, our deepest heart's intention for being at the retreat. Not the voice of the mind or the ego, but the truth that lives beneath it all. As I sat in stillness, the message from my experience under the moonlight came to me with clarity and softness. *"Be true to yourself and give yourself permission to receive your love."*

I understood then that the message was about more than just accepting yourself. It was about grace. The grace that asks for no striving, no fixing, no proving, only trust. Grace's simple allowance lets you rest, soften, and be whole as you are.

That night in India, under the vast sky, I felt a warmth rise through my chest, a quiet stillness settle in my belly, and an ease in my limbs, as if my body were finally exhaling. I was invited to trust, receive, and to step into the unknown, reminding me that I am already whole.

The clarity of this intention took my breath away, revealing for the first time how much I had spent years giving away what I most needed: grace, understanding, and kindness.

In the next breath, our teacher asked us what we were ready to release. It was the harsh inner critic that had long held space in my heart. I was exhausted. Exhausted from relentless self-judgement and the absence of self-compassion. Now, with this message resonating throughout my being, I no longer wanted to be cruel to myself. I yearned for a different way of being, a way of living with grace, moving through life with softness, compassion, and love for myself.

Under the moonlit skies of Tamil Nadu in India, *Embodied Grace: Trusting Yourself, Healing Deeply, Expanding Fully* was born. This sacred realisation is the foundation of this book and my hope for you.

You may have picked up this book because you, too, are ready to release the harsh judgements that have shaped your sense of self. Perhaps you've felt the burden of self-criticism, of striving to meet impossible standards, or of seeking approval from others in a way that leaves you feeling disconnected from your true essence. Or maybe you've come to these pages searching for a way to move through life with more compassion, authenticity, and grace.

Whatever led you here, my hope is that as you read these words, you'll find an invitation to shift your relationship with yourself. To embrace and embody grace, not as a distant ideal, but as a living, breathing practice that can transform how you experience the world and how you engage with your own heart.

May these pages remind you that grace already lives within you, waiting to be embodied through tenderness, trust, and love.

So much love, Stacey

How to Engage with this Book

These pages unfold, inviting you to meet yourself and awaken the grace that has always been within. This book is a journey, and across the eleven parts of this book, you are guided through the framework of Embodied Grace, exploring the sacred interplay between your mind, body, and spirit.

Each part weaves together wisdom, reflection, embodied insights, graceful reminders, and practices, creating space to trust yourself, heal deeply, and expand fully. These tools invite you to go beyond reading, helping you engage actively in your own healing and transformation and deepen your connection with yourself and the world around you.

Throughout these pages, I use terms like God, Divine, Infinite, Universe, and Spirit interchangeably. To me, they all reflect the same sacred truth: we are all one, we are all part of something greater. If these terms don't resonate with you, I invite you to choose language that feels authentic to your own connection with the sacred.

This book is designed to challenge you, stretch you, and take you out of your comfort zone. Embodied Grace is about growth and transformation, and with that comes the invitation to go deeper, to look inward, and to meet aspects of yourself that may have been overlooked or buried. While each chapter will encourage you to step into new spaces, you are invited to move at your own pace. It's perfectly okay to linger with one chapter for a while, allowing the practices, embodied insights, and shifts to integrate fully before moving on. Equally, you may feel the need to revisit a chapter and engage with it again.

At the end of some chapters, you will discover Embodied Insights, invitations for reflection. Take the time to sit with these prompts, allowing them to unfold naturally. The wisdom they reveal may surprise you. You will also find practices woven throughout, guiding you into deeper connection with your body, breath, and presence. These practices are potent portals to transformation. Engage with them fully and notice how they meet you exactly where you are.

Embodying grace is an active process. It asks for your presence, patience, and participation. Some moments may feel challenging or uncomfortable, yet each step, no matter how small, brings you closer to Embodied Grace.

Remember, growth and healing are nonlinear. Revisiting chapters or practices often reveals new insights and deeper understanding. Every return offers an opportunity to peel back another layer and embrace a fuller, more expansive . version of yourself.

By the end of this book, you will recognise your inherent worth and let grace guide you through each experience. Embodied Grace becomes a lived reality, grounded in your body and presence. This book is a companion, yet true wisdom has always been within you. Walk this path with curiosity, openness, and deep self-compassion.

PART ONE

The Initiation

The Arrival

There are moments in life that unfold within you and mark you forever. For me, that moment came under the moon in India. That image stayed with me, a reflection of something stirring within. A remembering of wholeness, even in the not-yet.

That night did not offer answers. It offered something softer. A message. One that would become the heartbeat of this book, an invitation to be true to myself and to finally receive the love I had long withheld from my heart. It was a message of grace.

I began to understand grace in a new way. Grace is the current that moves through life, soft yet powerful, unseen yet deeply felt. It lives in the pauses between breaths and the stillness between heartbeats. It arrives when we least expect it, often in the smallest gestures of love or the gentlest release of tension. Grace is the touch of tenderness that meets us when we are weary and the spaciousness that allows us to begin again. It is not something we earn or seek to deserve, but a presence that reminds us of our inherent worth. Grace moves through us like light through water, illuminating what is ready to be seen and softening what once felt unmovable.

People have described grace in many ways, through spiritual, philosophical, and somatic lenses. Often seen as a divine offering or a state of presence, it is also a way of moving through life with compassion and reverence.

Grace lives in the body, revealing itself in the way we anchor into safety, in the slowing of our breath when we feel held, and in the expansion that follows surrender. To embody grace is to be fully present, imperfect, and receptive to the tender rhythm of life moving through us. It is the movement of love that draws us home, unfolding in the spaces we allow ourselves to simply be.

Many traditions describe grace as a force that moves through life in both seen and unseen ways. In Hindu philosophy, grace is referred to as *kripa*, a divine blessing that flows when we surrender to the unfolding of life. Christian theology describes grace as an unmerited gift of love. Buddhist teachings, while not using the word 'grace,' speak of *karuna*, a deep compassion that arises naturally from presence and awareness. Across cultures and traditions, grace is recognised as a sacred force, one that nurtures, sustains, and expands.

As a white Australian, grace is something I understand, in part, from the Indigenous cultures of this land. The Aboriginal and Torres Strait Islander peoples speak of *spirit* and *connection* as elements of grace, where everything is interwoven—the people, land, skies, waters, and ancestors. Grace is found in the land's whispers, in listening to Country, and in the sacred relationship between humans and the Earth. It's grace that speaks of belonging, kinship, and the rhythms of nature, offering a reminder of reverence and humility.

I describe grace as a softening and a returning.

You might move through most days carrying invisible tension, the weight of always needing to hold everything together. Your shoulders are tight, your breath is shallow, and you do not even notice. It has simply become your normal.

Then something soft arrives.

A song plays, awakening a part of you long forgotten. Perhaps you step outside and feel the warmth of the sun land on your skin. Or you feel the embrace of someone you love, their touch carrying a message from God, reminding you that you are loved, held, and never alone.

You breathe, a deep, full, unexpected inhale followed by a surrendered exhale.

Your body remembers the softening, the surrender.

This is grace. It is what God feels like, a presence that does not come from outside of you but rises within the spaces you allow yourself to soften. Grace is the living essence of that sacred force found in presence, expressed through humility, and carried forward in loving action.

That exhale is the tension leaving your body, making space for grace to enter. That moment of dropping the armour is how grace becomes embodied. It is when your nervous system sighs, your heart and mind loosen their grip, and stillness settles into every fibre of you.

This is not a performance or a pursuit. It is a gentle return, a remembering of the wholeness that was never lost, only waiting to be felt again.

Grace allows us to stand in the light of self-compassion, to soften into the mystery of life, and to be guided by the wisdom already within us. In the rhythms of nature and the unfolding moments of our day, grace calls us to be present, to listen, and to honour the world within and around us. Grace is already here, in the softness of our being and the expansive potential of who we are becoming.

Embodied Insight
*What is arriving within you in this moment, and where in your
body can you feel it?*
Take a slow breath and notice what shifts as you simply allow it to be.

The Path of Embodied Grace

Grace is a deeply rooted way of being. The formula for cultivating Embodied Grace is simple yet profound, one that revealed itself to me through lived experience, intuitive guidance, and a deep listening to the body and spirit. It emerged as I navigated my healing, where presence, permission, and self-compassion became the pillars that held me. This is my formula for Embodied Grace:

Presence + Humility + Loving Action = Embodied Grace

These three pillars work together seamlessly, like threads woven into a fabric, creating a sense of balance and wholeness within ourselves and in our relationships with others. When integrated into our daily lives, they guide us toward living with self-compassion and grace.

Embodied Grace arises when presence, humility, and loving action unite. It is a sacred and ongoing practice, a living force that guides, supports, and empowers us to meet life with an open heart, a nourished nervous system, and deep connection.

This practice of Embodied Grace is not only transformative for our inner world, but it is also an energy that ripples outward, elevating our relationships, our communities, and all those we encounter. It becomes a wisdom of light, a sacred offering to the world around us. When we embody grace, we create space for others to do the same, creating environments where authenticity, kindness, and strength can flourish.

To guide you in cultivating this, we turn to the three pillars of Embodied Grace:

Presence grounds you. It anchors you in the here and now, enabling you to be fully alive in every moment. Presence opens the door to self-awareness, enabling you to navigate life with clarity and centeredness.

Humility opens your heart. Humility teaches you that we are all interconnected and we do not need to prove our worth or cling to the need for control. Humility softens the heart, allowing us to show up in vulnerability and embrace the divinity within others.

Loving action illuminates your path. Loving action goes beyond thought. It is the courage to act from a place of deep care, understanding, and purpose. It is expressed in the choices you make each day, small or large, that reflect compassion for yourself and others. This might be offering kindness without expectation, speaking your truth with honesty and gentleness, setting boundaries to protect your wellbeing, or moving through fear with intentional care. Loving action transforms your inner awareness into tangible gestures that nurture connection, build trust, and support growth. When guided by presence and humility, loving action becomes a force that aligns your heart, mind, and body, inviting grace into your life and the lives of those around you.

As you explore these pages, you will uncover the wisdom that the formula of presence, humility, and loving action offers in its highest expression. They serve as the pillars that hold you steady as you navigate your own path towards Embodied Grace.

You may already feel these qualities within you, as they are not new to your spirit and have always been part of your essence. As you move forward, let these three pillars be both your guide and your companions. They are not goals to achieve but invitations to trust yourself, to heal deeply, and to expand fully. Embodied Grace is alive within you, waiting to be noticed, nurtured, and expressed. In embracing it, you open yourself to the fullness of your being, to life's unfolding, and to the transformative power of living with an open heart.

Embodied Insight

What part of you is aware and present in this moment?
How does your heart feel when you allow yourself to soften without judgment?

Crying In The Corner

I first learnt my feelings could be 'too much' when I was eight or nine. I had worked harder on an assignment than I ever had before, and I felt proud, certain I would earn a high mark.

That morning at school, my chest sank as I realised I had left the assignment at home. All the hours of work, all the hope I had carried, had disappeared in an instant. My throat tightened, my eyes filled, and by the time I got to the playground, the tears were running down my face.

A teacher saw me and came over. For a moment, I thought she might understand, that she might tell me it would be all right. Instead, she looked at me and said sharply, "Stop crying, Stacey. You're being silly." Her words cut deeper than forgetting the assignment. She wasn't just dismissing my mistake. She was dismissing me. My emotions were wrong. I was wrong.

She put me in a corner of the playground and told me to stay there until I stopped crying. No one was allowed to come near me. I pressed my back against the cold wall and listened to the sound of children laughing and shouting as they played, while I stood alone, my cheeks burning and tears I could no longer wipe away. Whenever a student walked toward me, she shouted from across the playground for them to leave me alone until I stopped being silly.

I thought I had done something terribly wrong, that my feelings made me bad and that crying made me unworthy of kindness. I tried to swallow my tears, hoping that would make it stop, that I could be good again.

It took years before I understood what that moment had taught me. Emotions were not safe. If I allowed them to surface, I would be punished, isolated, and shamed.

That belief followed me into adulthood and into my years as a police officer. In a world where composure and toughness were expected, I carried the same shame. Anytime tears would threaten, I forced them back.

I can still remember returning to my police car after delivering my first death message. The family's screams pierced through me, raw with grief, ringing in my ears long after I walked away. Sitting in the driver's seat, the silence pressed in. My chest heaved as tears pushed forward, but I swallowed them down. My hands gripped the steering wheel until my knuckles turned white. I hated myself for even feeling them.

As I sat there fighting back tears, I realised I was doing what I had always done. The little girl in the playground had learnt to hide her feelings to be safe, and the woman in uniform was still following the same rule. I straightened my uniform, called in the update on the police radio with a voice that sounded steady but felt hollow, and shifted my gaze to the horizon, refusing to look at my reflection in the window before I started driving. When my colleague asked if I was okay, I smiled and said I was fine. Then I turned up the radio, flooded the car with noise, and focused on the next job. That was how I dismissed what I felt. By moving on quickly, hiding behind humour and work, and pretending I was unaffected. I learnt to numb through doing.

I never returned to those feelings. I tucked them deep within me, folded into the fabric of my body where they could not be seen. Each unacknowledged ache settled quietly inside, waiting for a moment of safety that never came. I told myself I was strong, but really, I had just become skilled at turning away from my tenderness.

It took years before I understood how deeply that playground moment had shaped me. I had been taught to dismiss my emotions instead of honouring them. I had been conditioned to believe that my body was betraying me whenever it revealed the truth of what I was feeling.

The turning point came in my twenties when I began my healing journey. I was sick of the relentless voice in my head telling me I wasn't enough. I would meet each day striving, achieving and pleasing, all while my body tightened and my heart dimmed. In the heaviness of that exhaustion, something inside me longs for another way to be with myself.

It was grace that taught me to slow down. To soften instead of harden, to listen instead of suppressing, and to hold myself with compassion instead of criticism. I would often picture the little girl in the playground, tears still wet on her cheeks. I would cradle her in my arms, whispering what no one had told her then. "You are safe. You are seen. Your feelings are enough." I came to understand my tears were not weakness but wisdom. That my body was not my enemy but my ally. True strength was never about never breaking. It was about meeting the breaking with kindness.

This is what I mean when I speak of Embodied Grace. It is more than this story, though this story was one of my doorways into it. Embodied Grace is a way of living with compassion for ourselves in every moment. It is the courage to allow what once felt unacceptable. It is the steady practice of trusting our body's wisdom, even when the world tells us to silence it. Embodied Grace is the reminder that grace is not earned through perfection but revealed in presence.

Even now, when the echoes rise and I remember the sting of shame on that playground or the piercing screams of grief in the night, I return to grace. Embodied Grace is what I learnt through countless initiations, moments when life challenged me, when my body and emotions demanded to be seen, and when I was called to respond with compassion rather than judgement. And grace always whispers the truth I could not hear back then. "You are enough, just as you are."

Graceful Reminder
Feeling fully is never weakness. It is the path to your own grace.

Threshold

You stand at the threshold,
not of something beyond you,
but of your own return.

You choose to show up.
You feel.
You listen.
You stay.

With this choice, you begin the journey of Embodied Grace.
You meet yourself with presence.
You bring tenderness to each breath.
You honour your timing and your truth.

As you step forward, you trust your body to guide you.
Let your heart lead with gentleness.
Let your spirit remind you that you are never alone.

You carry grace within you.
And now, you live it.

A Call to Yourself

After years of silencing my tears and pushing down my emotions, I began a journey to meet myself differently. I started noticing the small, quiet ways my body carried the weight of my feelings the tightness in my chest, the tension in my shoulders, the flutter of nerves when trying something new. I realised the emotions I had been taught to hide—grief, fear, longing, even joy, were not my enemies. They were messengers, guiding me back to myself, calling me to pay attention and listen.

You have picked up this book for a reason. You are here because part of you is ready to trust yourself, to heal deeply, and to expand fully. Perhaps you have been carrying old wounds, memories of moments when your feelings were dismissed, or the lingering echo of shame telling you that your emotions are too much. I invite you to notice these feelings without judgement and to hold them gently. They are part of your story, part of your life, and part of the journey toward Embodied Grace.

As I reflect on my path, and on the shift that began for me in that quiet, moonlit space in India, I feel a deep desire to invite you into your own experience. This is your moment to connect with your own sankalpa, your heartfelt intention for your time with this book. This intention is yours and yours alone. It may come as a word, a feeling, a gentle whisper from deep within. It is the first step in trusting yourself, embracing your own capacity to heal deeply, and stepping into the grace and expansion that already lives within you.

Practice: Setting Your Sankalpa

Find a seat that feels safe and comfortable. Let your spine lengthen gently and your shoulders soften, noticing what feels easy rather than forcing a posture. If it feels safe, bring your hands in front of your heart, palms open and facing upwards. You can lightly touch the edges of your little fingers together, keeping your hands softly cupped, as if holding something precious. If that doesn't feel right, simply rest your hands wherever feels natural.

Take a slow, full breath in through your nose. Exhale with a gentle sigh through your mouth, releasing tension. This hand position, the Receptivity Mudra, invites you to receive life's gifts and meet yourself with gentle acceptance.

Close your eyes or soften your gaze and turn your attention inward. Let your heart settle and ask yourself:
What do I truly seek in this moment?
What am I ready to welcome or release?
What intention feels most authentic to carry forward on this journey toward embodied grace?

Notice how the answers arise—a feeling, a word, an image, or quiet knowing. There is no right or wrong way.

When you feel ready, gently place your hands over your heart and take three slow breaths, inhaling through your nose and exhaling with a soft sigh. Thank yourself for this moment of connection.

Finally, release your hands. If you wish, jot down whatever came through. Carry this intention with you, returning to it whenever you need, letting it guide your path with an open heart.

A Message from Your Soul

You have opened your heart.
You have listened.
You have set your intention.

The truth has always been within you, alive and radiant.
It is yours to feel, yours to trust, and yours to embody.

You are whole.
You are worthy.
You are love.

Trust yourself.
Feel deeply.
Step fully into your grace.

Every breath, every heartbeat, is a reminder,
You are exactly where you need to be.

PART TWO

The Language of Your Body

Your Body's Sacred Signal

Long before I knew about the nervous system, I noticed subtle signals from my body. Some mornings I would wake with heaviness in my chest, tight shoulders, and shallow breath, urging me to pay attention. Other times, my body swelled with energy, my heart lifted, or a sense of ease and curiosity spread through me, inviting me to move, explore, or simply be present. These were signals from my body, guiding me toward presence, awareness, and care.

At first, I often ignored these messages, thinking I had to push on. I would tell myself I was fine, that the tension or fluttering was just in my head. I carried the weight of expectation, of needing to appear capable and strong, even when every part of me whispered to slow down. Looking back, I can see that every sensation was a signal from my body, showing me the way.

Over time, I recognised these signals as protective and expansive. The flutter in my stomach before a difficult conversation, the lift in my chest when something felt aligned, the tension in my hands before making a choice. Each was meaningful if I paused long enough to notice. When I listened, I felt supported and more connected to myself and the world. When I ignored them, I carried discomfort quietly throughout my day.

This is your invitation to reconnect with your body, to notice its signals without judgement, and to honour the wisdom it has been offering all along. Your body is not just a vessel. It is a teacher, a guide, and a sacred map leading you toward awareness, presence, and care.

Graceful Reminder

*Every sensation is a message, every breath a teacher. Your body carries
the language of your life.*

The Silent Power Behind Your Life

As a young police officer back in 2006, I didn't give much thought to the term nervous system. If you had asked me then, I would have said it was just the thing that kept my heart beating and my lungs breathing without me having to think about it. And sure, that is part of the picture. The autonomic nervous system is the behind-the-scenes operator that keeps the body functioning, regulating our heart rate, digestion, and breathing automatically.

What I didn't realise at the time was how much this silent powerhouse shaped not only my body, but also my emotions, decisions, and sense of safety in the world.

Working with victims and witnesses gave me my first clues. They needed to feel safe enough to share raw and vulnerable details. Without that sense of safety, memories often became fragmented, and details were held back in fear. In moments of urgency, like rushing to grab a child's hand, the body moves faster than thought. Survival takes over, narrowing focus, silencing reflection, and holding back words that might otherwise be spoken once safety returns. At the same time, I noticed how differently my colleagues and I responded to chaos. One person would freeze while another lashed out. I could stay composed one moment yet feel utterly overwhelmed the next.

The detective in me wondered, Why do we react the way we do? What shapes these responses?

Over time, the pattern became undeniable. Our nervous systems were running the show, mine included. There were nights of hypervigilance when my body was wired with adrenaline, ready to respond in an instant, and days when exhaustion sank deep into my bones. Even in moments of quiet, my body carried the aftershocks of what I had witnessed.

As I started to connect the dots, I came to see that the autonomic nervous system does far more than regulate the heart and lungs. It shapes how we feel, think, and respond. Stress clouds judgement. Certain sights or sounds can trigger us before we even realise it, and old protective patterns can quietly keep us stuck.

That growing curiosity led me to over a decade of studying the nervous system, trauma, and somatic work. What I discovered changed everything. The nervous system is not just about survival. It is a living, sensing part of us that guides connection, supports healing, invites grace, and opens the way to expansion.

Understanding this begins with knowing the two main branches of the autonomic nervous system.

The language used in this book reflects several frameworks used to understand autonomic nervous system states. It is offered as a practical lens, not an exhaustive explanation of the nervous system's complexity.

The Sympathetic Nervous System is the body's accelerator. It activates when we perceive danger, releasing adrenaline to prepare us for action, whether fight or flight. It sharpens focus, heightens awareness, and fuels energy for immediate response. Think of slamming on the brakes to avoid a car, rushing to grab a child's hand before they step into danger, or stepping away from confrontation.

The Parasympathetic Nervous System is the body's brake pedal. It helps us rest, recover, and return to balance. It includes the ventral vagal pathway, our state of safety and social connection, and the dorsal vagal pathway, which can trigger freeze, disconnection, or shutdown under overwhelming stress.

The balance between these branches shapes how we move through life. Are we energised or depleted, open-hearted or withdrawn, safe or on edge? Understanding these states allows us to meet ourselves with awareness and gently bring ourselves back into connection.

Learning about my nervous system began long before I became an intuitive somatic mentor. As a police officer, I carried the weight of hypervigilance, adrenaline spikes, and unspoken responsibility. My body was tense, my jaw tight, shoulders rigid, chest heavy, and rest felt impossible. I strived for perfection, over-prepared for every call, and avoided vulnerability to appear strong. My mind replayed incidents long after they ended, while my body quietly held the stress.

For years, I simply survived. But eventually, I realised that if I wanted to trust myself, heal, and expand in life, I had to do more than understand the nervous system. I had to work with it.

Working somatically means connecting with the wisdom of your body, listening to its signals, and understanding what they are communicating about your emotional and physical state. When we recognise we are stuck in survival mode, we can guide ourselves back to safety and connection within. Healing is not about forcing calm. It is about supporting the nervous system to feel safe enough to meet discomfort, release old patterns, and return to its natural rhythm.

Our nervous system is the rhythm behind our emotions, our thoughts, and our capacity for joy, connection, and presence. When we learn to understand and work with it, we hold the key to transforming not only our wellbeing but also the way we move through the world.

Graceful Reminder

In the rhythm of your nervous system lies the grace to heal, grow, and expand. When you learn to honour its cues, you unlock the door to transformation.

The States Within

Our nervous system continually shapes how we experience life, influencing our sense of safety, our responses to stress, and our capacity for connection. By noticing its different states and how they show up in the body, we can recognise the wisdom in our responses and support ourselves in whichever state we find ourselves in.

Ventral Vagal State (Safety and Connection)
The ventral vagal pathway supports feelings of safety, calm, and connection. It allows us to engage meaningfully with others, cultivate joy, and form social bonds. According to Deb Dana[1], a deep sense of belonging, connection to oneself, openness to change, and the ability to reach out and explore new possibilities are all part of this central state. Being in a ventral vagal state allows you to feel safe, present, and open to life. It is the foundation for resilience, enabling you to meet challenges with grace and adaptability. This state nurtures creativity, problem-solving, and deeper relationships, as self-compassion flows naturally when the body and mind are in harmony.

After years of learning to notice and support my nervous system, I sought moments that allowed me to embody safety and connection fully. One of the simplest and most profound ways I do this is in my backyard, sitting beneath the shade of my Jacaranda tree.

I lean against its sturdy trunk, feeling the rough texture of the bark against my back. The branches stretch above me, their delicate purple blossoms whispering in the breeze. Sunlight filters through the leaves, casting shifting patterns on the ground and on my skin. Each breath I take slows, each exhale releasing tension I didn't realise I had been carrying.

The air smells faintly of earth and flowers, and I notice the gentle rhythm of life all around me. Birds call softly from the branches, their song weaving into the rustle of leaves. My shoulders soften, my chest opens, and my mind quiets. The worries, pressures, and self-judgements I carried moments before dissolve, replaced by a deep sense of ease and groundedness.

I notice the rise and fall of my breath, the pulse of my body against the trunk, and the steady heartbeat of the earth beneath me. In this stillness, I feel fully present, fully supported, fully alive. Joy surfaces quietly, insights emerge naturally, and self-compassion flows without effort. Sitting here, leaning against the Jacaranda, I am held—by the tree, by my body, and by life itself.

This is the ventral vagal state in action: a place of safety, presence, and connection, where the nervous system relaxes, and the heart, mind, and body align. It is here, leaning against my Jacaranda, that I remember what it feels like to be fully held by myself and to move through life with ease and grace.

Sympathetic State (Fight or Flight)
The sympathetic nervous system activates when the body perceives a threat. It prepares us to respond quickly, either to fight danger or to flee from it. In fight, the body tenses, muscles tighten, the jaw may clench, the chest feels heavy or tight, and thoughts race with urgency or anger. In flight, the body may feel restless, the heart races, breathing becomes rapid, and there is a strong impulse to run, hide, or escape. These responses are essential for survival, but when they are triggered too often, or when danger is no longer present, the body can feel perpetually on edge. Chronic activation can lead to exhaustion, anxiety, irritability, and disconnection from oneself and others.

One of my clients, Jennifer, often experienced *fight*. She noticed a tightness in her chest, clenched jaw, and thoughts spinning before she even realised she was reacting. Minor frustrations at work felt like emergencies. Her body braced for conflict, her mind prepared arguments, and her chest burned with tension. Even when no threat existed, her nervous system remained on high alert, making it difficult to soften, respond with patience, or notice her own needs.

Through our work together, Jennifer learnt to pause and notice the signals her body was sending. She realised that her fight response was actually a message that she was overworked, suppressing feelings, and neglecting boundaries. By attending to these needs—breathing, moving, speaking her truth—her nervous system gradually returned to connection within, and she could respond with clarity instead of reactivity.

Another client, Emily, often experienced *flight*. In social situations, she felt an overwhelming urge to escape. Her heart raced, her breath became shallow, and her muscles tensed with the anticipation of running away. Thoughts spun rapidly. I need to leave. I do not belong. I cannot handle this. Even when she knew intellectually that the situation was safe, her body behaved as though danger was imminent. She would seek the nearest exit, avoid eye contact, or distract herself with work.

Exploring this together, Emily traced the pattern back to childhood. She remembered a moment of embarrassment and being ignored in a social setting. Her body learnt then that the safest choice was to retreat. For years, her nervous system rehearsed that strategy automatically, triggering flight at even small discomforts.

Rather than forcing herself to stay or pushing through, Emily began to witness the response with curiosity. She noticed the racing heart, the tight stomach, and the restlessness in her limbs. Instead of dismissing it, she gently acknowledged the younger part of her that had once needed to escape. She imagined the embarrassed child who felt unseen and alone and inwardly let her know she was no longer facing it by herself. With warmth rather than judgment, she stayed present to the sensations, almost as if sitting beside that younger Emily. Rather than insisting she was safe, she offered steadiness. I am here. We can go slowly. Over time, her body began to register this new experience. She discovered she could remain in social interactions, not by overriding the urge to flee, but by tending to the part that once needed to.

This is the sympathetic state in action, a body primed for survival, sometimes long after the danger has passed. By noticing and acknowledging the signals, we can meet our nervous system with curiosity and support its needs where the nervous system naturally brings itself back into safety and connection within.

Dorsal Vagal State (Freeze, Shutdown and/or Disconnection)
The dorsal vagal state is activated when the body perceives a threat as too overwhelming to manage. In this state, the parasympathetic nervous system triggers a freeze or shutdown response. Numbness, disconnection, heaviness, and helplessness characterise it. While this response can be protective in moments of

extreme stress, prolonged time here can leave us feeling isolated, depleted, and disengaged from ourselves and the world around us.

My client, Beth, was often unable to respond in moments of confrontation. Whether it was a difficult conversation with a loved one or an unexpected challenge at work, she would suddenly feel frozen. Her mind blanked, her body grew heavy, and her breath became shallow. She described it as feeling stuck, unable to think clearly or take action, even when she wanted to.

Growing up in an unpredictable household, Beth's nervous system had learned to scan constantly for sudden changes in tone, mood, or atmosphere. She never knew when warmth might turn into anger, or calm into chaos. Over time, her body learnt that the safest option was to become small, quiet, and invisible. In adulthood, even minor conflict carried the echo of that unpredictability. A raised voice, a sharp email, an unexpected question, her system reacted as though the ground beneath her might disappear again. The freeze was not weakness; it was an old strategy shaped in an environment where unpredictability meant risk.

Rather than trying to push through the freeze, Beth learnt to recognise the early signs that it was beginning. She noticed the subtle tightening in her throat, the heaviness behind her eyes, the way her thoughts started to scatter and disappear. Instead of criticising herself for "shutting down," she practised pausing internally and naming what was happening: *My body is trying to protect me.*

At first, the work was small. She would gently press her feet into the floor and feel the support beneath her. She would lengthen her exhale, not to force calm, but to create a little more space inside the moment. Sometimes she would place a hand over her chest or rest her palm on her thigh, offering her body a signal of anchoring. These simple anchors helped her stay in contact with herself, even when part of her wanted to disappear.

Outside of confrontation, we built capacity slowly. Through resourcing practices, reflective journalling, and safe relational experiences in our sessions, her nervous system began to learn that presence did not always equal danger. She wasn't trying to override the freeze; she was widening her window of tolerance so that activation no longer tipped her into shutdown quite so quickly.

Over time, something shifted. There were moments in difficult conversations where she still felt the familiar wave of heaviness, but she no longer disappeared into it. She could sense what was happening in her body and gently invite connection within the shutdown itself. Her thoughts returned more quickly. Her breath deepened. Her voice, once lost, began to stay with her.

Another client, Lisa, experienced dorsal vagal shutdown when life felt too overwhelming. When work pressures piled up or personal challenges became too much, she would withdraw, sleep for long hours, avoid messages from friends, and feel disconnected from her own emotions. She described it as if a fog had settled over her, making it hard to care about anything.

Growing up in a household where support felt inconsistent, Lisa's nervous system had learned early on that retreat and stillness were safer than reaching out. Even small signs of pressure in adulthood, a tight deadline, a difficult conversation, or an unreturned message, could trigger the same protective response. Her body was simply doing what it had been trained to do, keeping her safe.

Rather than forcing herself to snap out of it, Lisa began to notice the signals of shutdown, the heaviness in her chest, the fog in her mind, the slowing of her breath, and meet them with compassion. She placed a hand on her chest, allowed herself to breathe into the tightness, and gently explored small ways to reconnect with her body and surroundings. She also began taking small steps to receive support from others, allowing herself to respond to a friend's message, ask for help with a work task, or simply accept company when she needed it. She did not try to push the shutdown away; she learned to invite awareness and connection within it.

Over time, Lisa discovered that these small, intentional steps helped her move through shutdown moments more smoothly. She could feel her presence returning, her attention settling, and her thoughts coming back into focus. Gradually, she began to respond to challenges with clarity, engagement, and a sense of grounded connection, even in moments that previously would have left her completely withdrawn.

Even in the dorsal vagal state, the body is trying to protect and guide us. When we notice these moments without judgement, we can listen to what our nervous system needs. Each pause, each shutdown, carries information about what feels unsafe and what might help us return to presence. With time and awareness, these states can become a doorway to reconnecting with ourselves, our bodies, and the world around us.

Understanding the Fawn State

You may have heard of the fight, flight, freeze, and fawn responses and wondered where fawn fits in. Fawning is a unique survival strategy and a blended state involving either sympathetic (fight-or-flight) or dorsal vagal (freeze, shutdown, or disconnection) activation.

In the fawn state, sympathetic activation heightens our hypervigilance. We become acutely attuned to others' cues, behaviours, and actions, often monitoring for shifts that could signal danger or conflict. This hyper-awareness drives us to appease or placate others, sometimes through people-pleasing, to anticipate and avoid harm.

When combined with dorsal vagal activation, the fawn state can disconnect us from our own feelings, values, and inner energy. We may give away our power, submitting to those who hold or misuse authority. This can leave us dissociated, abdicating our autonomy, and adopting people-pleasing behaviours to avoid confrontation. Over time, this can lead to a loss of self, where decisions and actions are no longer aligned with who we truly are.

My client, Olivia had spent most of her life prioritizing the needs and emotions of others, often at the expense of her own. In friendships, relationships, and at work, she would go out of her way to keep the peace, agreeing to things she didn't want, suppressing her opinions, and constantly reading the moods of those around her to avoid conflict. She described feeling exhausted and unseen, yet the thought of asserting herself filled her with anxiety.

Growing up in a home where expressing her needs led to criticism or rejection, Olivia's nervous system had learned that being agreeable was the safest option. She had adapted by making herself as unobtrusive as possible. Even in adulthood, the habit persisted, leaving her disconnected from her own needs and desires.

Rather than trying to force herself to be more assertive overnight, Olivia began by noticing the familiar flutter in her stomach, the hesitation in her voice, and the subtle tension in her jaw whenever she was about to abandon her own wants. She placed a hand on her heart, slowed her breath, and allowed herself to pause and feel what she truly needed.

She also took small, manageable steps to express herself and receive support from others. At first, it was simple things, like replying to a colleague's message honestly instead of automatically saying yes, or letting a friend know she needed a listening ear. She practiced asking for help in low-stakes moments, noticing the flutter in her stomach and the hesitation in her voice, and then gently taking the step anyway. Sometimes she would rehearse what to say quietly to herself, or write a short note explaining what she needed. Each time she reached out, she reinforced that it was safe to rely on others and that her needs mattered. She did not push past the discomfort; she invited awareness and connection within the moments when she felt compelled to fawn.

Over time, Olivia discovered that these small, intentional steps strengthened her sense of self. She could stay present in interactions, speak her truth, and maintain meaningful relationships without losing herself. Gradually, she began to act from her own values and desires, reclaiming her autonomy while still staying connected to those around her.

Like fight, flight, and freeze, the fawn state is a survival response and your body's intelligent way of keeping you safe when it senses a threat. While it may have once protected you, it can become a default pattern that limits authentic living and self-connection.

There is nothing bad or wrong if you find yourself in a sympathetic or dorsal vagal state. These states are not failures. They are intelligent, protective energies flowing through your nervous system. To me, there is no hierarchy here. One state is not better than another. They are simply different expressions of your system, moving and responding to keep you safe in the only way it knows how.

It is also important to remember that we are rarely in just one state. The nervous system is dynamic. In everyday life, we often move between states or hold elements of more than one at the same time. You might feel anxious and exhausted. Activated and disconnected. Open in one moment and guarded in the next. This is not confusion. It is complexity. It is being human.

When we begin to recognise the energy we are in, something shifts. Awareness softens the edges. It creates space between who we are and what we are experiencing.

If sympathetic activation is present, you may notice urgency, heat, anger, anxiety, or the push to act immediately. In this activation, you can support the energy rather than shame it. You can allow the anger to be felt without letting it take over. You can move the energy instead of turning it against yourself.

If dorsal patterns are moving through you, you may feel heaviness, numbness, shutdown, or a sense of collapse. Here, the invitation is tenderness. You can meet yourself slowly. You can bring warmth to what feels distant. You can offer presence where there has been pressure.

While these are described separately for clarity, they often overlap in lived experience. Awareness creates choice. And from that place, we can begin to invite regulation, compassion, safety, and connection. Not by forcing ourselves into a better state, but by honouring the energy we are in.

Graceful Reminder
Each state of your nervous system holds wisdom. Awareness is the doorway to healing and inner safety.

Where Love Still Lives

When I was twelve years old, my dad died by suicide. Even before anyone told me, I intuitively knew he had passed.

The day of his funeral is still vivid in my memory. I was asked if I wanted to see him, and I said yes immediately. I needed to see him to believe it because part of me was still hoping this was a nightmare I could wake from. I was led into the room, and there he was, lying in the casket. He was dressed in a suit, which felt strange. Dad never wore suits. He was usually in his singlet and stubby shorts.

I wanted to touch his hand, to reach out and connect, but I could not. I was frozen. My chest tightened, my stomach churned, and my breath became shallow. My body seemed to understand the enormity of what was happening before my mind could even grasp it. Looking back now, I recognise this as my nervous system at work. My vagus nerve, the wandering nerve that carries signals between brain and body, had already kicked in. My body was sending urgent messages to my brain, orchestrating my body's freeze response, keeping me intact in the face of something too vast to comprehend.

Everything felt magnified. Every shiver, every rush of heat, every tightening in my chest was a message from my body. This is huge. This is overwhelming. Protect yourself. The next thing I remember is sitting in the funeral. I have no memory of leaving the open casket. My dorsal vagal pathways were fully engaged, helping me survive a moment my mind could not yet name.

For years I carried the regret of not touching him, of not holding his hand. I remembered our last conversation. He had said he loved me, but I could not recall the last time I had held his hand. Now, in understanding the nervous system, I see that my body was doing exactly what it needed to do. That freeze, the shallow breath, the tight chest—they were protective measures, not failures. They allowed me to process the shock slowly, to survive the grief before I could fully feel it.

Learning to listen to my body, to honour its signals and offer it care, has shown me that healing often begins there. My nervous system was working all along, helping me survive even when I felt frozen and disconnected. Now I can offer myself grace for that moment, for the fear, the hesitation, and the hands I did not hold. I can acknowledge that my body was protecting me, and in that recognition I find compassion for myself. Grace is the gentle acceptance that I did the best I could in the face of something too vast to bear.

Now, every time I remember this memory, I am reminded of other memories too. Holding his hand to cross the road safely as a child, giving each other a high 5 when something went right in the world, and now I realise that even in my grief, those simple touches were seeds of grace, guiding me back to connection.

Graceful Reminder

Grace is not about what you did or did not do, but about honouring the body and heart that carried you through.

Support and Nourishment

Support and nourishment for our nervous system can take many forms. It might be a mindful breath, a slow walk, a moment in nature, or simply noticing sensations in your body with curiosity and compassion. It might include connecting with others in co-regulation, sharing a calm presence, or engaging in practices that help your nervous system feel seen, safe, and held.

When we speak of self-regulation or co-regulation, the intention is not to quickly move back into the ventral vagal state or to override what you are feeling. You do not want to bypass your emotions or sensations. Instead, these practices invite awareness of where you are, understanding why your body might respond the way it is, and offering yourself the support you need in that moment. Regulation is not about fixing or forcing. It is about witnessing, listening, tending, soothing, expanding and co-creating with the universe.

Self-Regulation
Self-regulation is the practice of supporting and nourishing your nervous system, allowing it to naturally return to balance and ease within the ventral vagal state. Think of it as a personal toolkit, filled with resources you can reach for when you wish to re-establish and cultivate safety from within.

Some of the most common self-regulation techniques include:

Rest and sleep: Allows your nervous system to recover, recharge, and strengthen its ability to support you throughout the day.

Breathwork: Supports your nervous system to move toward openness and ease, supporting overall balance.

Emotional Freedom Techniques (EFT or Tapping): An empowering practice that supports the rewiring of the nervous system using gentle pressure points.

Shaking: Shaking off stress helps release stored tension in the body.

Exercise: Moving your body stimulates endorphins and supports the nervous system.

Connecting with nature: The grounding energy of nature can help reset our entire system.

Meditation: A powerful practice to find peace and clarity.

Deep sighs: A simple release of built-up tension.

Humming, deep sighs, singing, chanting, or laughing: All stimulate the vagus nerve and help strengthen vagal tone, supporting nervous system regulation.

Mindfulness: Staying present can help your nervous system feel steady, supported, and responsive.

Finding fun and exciting ways to move your body: Dancing, stretching, or playful movement can release stress and increase joy.

Heart congruence: Connecting with your heart to feel aligned and centred.

Gentle touch: Reassuring yourself with self-compassionate touch.

Listening to music: Influences your nervous system, helping to soothe, uplift, and bring a sense of harmony and balance.

You can weave these practices into your day, whether you're feeling supported or navigating a stressful moment. They allow you to honour your nervous system and keep yourself nurtured and nourished in whatever state you're in.

The practices shared throughout this book will gently incorporate many of these self-regulation tools, inviting you to explore them through an intuitive somatic lens. As you move through each chapter, you'll have opportunities to engage with these practices not just as techniques, but as living experiences that support your journey of Embodied Grace.

Co-Regulation

Co-regulation is the deeply human and natural process of finding regulation in the presence of others. Our bodies are wired for connection, and sometimes, simply being with someone who is grounded, present, and attuned can help guide us back to our own sense of balance. Just as a gentle breeze helps the leaves on a tree settle, the steady presence of another can help us feel safe, supported, and at ease.

Many of the same self-regulation practices I mentioned above can be done together with others, allowing you to experience co-regulation. For example, you might practice breathwork or meditation together, take a nature walk, or simply share a peaceful moment with a loved one. When we're in the presence of others—whether it's a trusted friend, a group, or even animals or nature—we can co-regulate and feel supported in our healing journey.

In addition to the practices mentioned in self-regulation, co-regulation might look like:

- Sitting with a trusted friend or loved one, simply being present with one another.

- Attending a support circle or group event can be a beautiful way to connect with like-minded people. You'll find a list of supportive and recommended resources, including my upcoming circles and events, at the back of this book.

- Joining group mindfulness or meditation sessions to tap into collective connection.

- Participating in grounding embodied practices such as yoga, nature walks, or gentle movement with others.

- Holding hands or sharing physical touch with someone (with consent), which can be incredibly soothing.

- Being in the presence of animals or nature, both of which have a natural calming effect on the nervous system.

The beauty of both self-regulation and co-regulation is that they're tools you can use at any time. Whether you're alone, with a loved one, or in a group, these practices support you in finding safety, grounding, and connection. They're opportunities to show up for yourself with kindness and compassion.

I've seen firsthand the power of these practices when my clients integrate them into their daily lives. Many of my clients receive simple, yet profound practices between sessions, tools that are gentle and supportive, related to our session. These practices might be a short breathwork exercise, a moment of mindfulness, or compassionate touch. They're designed to be doable in the flow of daily life, offering a space for either self-regulation or co-regulation, depending on what feels right in the moment.

People who join my group spaces often find them deeply nurturing, offering a supportive environment for co-regulation. There's something so powerful about coming together with others who understand the importance of supporting their nervous systems. Just sitting in the shared space, engaging in a calming practice together, or even just being present with others, can create a sense of safety and belonging that helps reset and rebalance our nervous systems. What I've observed is that it's not just the big moments of crisis that require attention to our nervous systems, but the everyday moments of feeling safe and connected too. It's easy to overlook how important it is to continue nourishing our nervous systems even when we're feeling grounded. But just like tending to a garden, if we only pay attention to our plants when they're wilting, it takes more time and effort to bring them back to health. By practising self-regulation and co-regulation when we're feeling connected, we continue nourishing our nervous system, preventing burnout and stress down the road.

Another beautiful thing I've seen is how these practices ripple out into our communities. My clients often begin using these tools not just for themselves, but with their friends, children, and loved ones. The practices they've learnt start to create positive ripples in the field, spreading the benefits of nervous system regulation beyond just their own experience. Whether it's introducing a child to breathing exercises or practising mindfulness with a partner, these tools become a way to create shared moments of connection and calm that uplift everyone involved.

So, whether you're practising self-regulation in a moment by yourself or joining a co-regulation practice with others, remember that these tools are your allies in creating connection and safety within. They are not only for when you're feeling overwhelmed but are vital practices to weave into your life, every single day. This ongoing journey of tending to yourself. One practice. One breath at a time, is how we create lasting grounding, connection, and resilience. And as you continue to nurture and nourish your nervous system, you'll notice the ripple effects it has, reaching out to those you care about and beyond.

Embodied Insight

How can you begin to incorporate self-regulation practices into your daily life, even when you feel connected? What tools resonate with you the most, and how can you weave them into your routine?

In what ways have you experienced the benefits of co-regulation? How does being with others in a calming environment affect your nervous system, and how can you create more of these opportunities in your life?

When the Body Speaks

A few years ago, a passing comment from a colleague about one of my police investigations caught me off guard. My chest tightened, my heart raced, and a wave of defensiveness washed over me. At first, I had no idea why, only that I felt a surge of anger toward him. It wasn't until later, when I paused and asked myself with curiosity why I was reacting so strongly, that some clarity emerged. I realised his tone echoed a past encounter, one filled with criticism and dismissal from someone else. My body reacted as it had originally when it sensed danger, even though he meant no harm.

Danger can be imminent, perceived, imagined, or remembered, and the nervous system signals the brain to protect the body. Right then, my nervous system was speaking drawing on old patterns shaped by fear: fear that I was not a good investigator, fear of judgement, fear of failing. These fears had nothing to do with the comment itself, yet my body responded automatically.

This is dysregulation in action: the fight, flight, freeze, or fawn responses. My chest tightness was fight preparing me to defend. My mind raced through worst-case scenarios, the subtle shadow of flight. Part of me wanted to shut down, freeze, disappear into the background. And the fawn, trying to appease, to prove I belonged, to avoid conflict, whispered its familiar story.

The nervous system does not understand time. It lives entirely in the present, scanning endlessly for cues of safety or threat, mobilising the body to protect you. It responds instinctively, as it always has, drawing from memories, fears, and past experiences.

Over time, I learnt to meet these moments with curiosity rather than judgement. I ask myself often, What is my nervous system trying to tell me? Am I reacting to now, or to another experience? When I pause and remind myself, I am safe in this moment, the tightness softens, the racing slows, and I find my body grounded again.

It's important to remember that dysregulation is not inherently bad. It is a messenger. The body is showing you where safety, boundaries, or attention is needed. It signals what has been unhealed, unmet, or unacknowledged. In this sense, each wave of dysregulation is a doorway to insight, growth, and deeper connection with yourself.

Practice: Nervous System Check-In

Find a comfortable space where you can be present with yourself. Take a few deep breaths, letting your body settle into the moment.

Gently ask, "What is my nervous system trying to tell me right now?" Notice any sensations, emotions, or thoughts. Is there heaviness, lightness, tension, or ease? Observe without judgement.

Then with curiosity, ask, "Am I responding to what's happening right now or is this a reaction to another experience?" Take a moment to reflect. Do these sensations belong to the present moment, or do they carry the weight of something past? Perhaps a tightness, a flutter, or a heaviness is carrying a memory, a protective pattern, a story from the past. Let it surface without judgement.

Stay with your breath. Feel the rhythm of your body. Place a hand on your heart or on your belly if it helps you feel supported. Allow yourself to meet whatever arises with gentle curiosity and care.

Notice how your body responds as you offer this attention. Perhaps a subtle shift, a softening, a release, a confirmation that your nervous system has been heard.

Take a final, slow breath and let your body settle into this moment. Know that simply noticing and listening has offered your nervous system acknowledgment and care. When you're ready, carry this awareness with you, moving forward with a sense of presence, ease, and gentle curiosity.

Screening Phone Calls

When the twins started kindergarten, my husband, Grant, and I experienced
a mix of excitement and nervousness. After nearly a decade of daycare, all our
children were finally in school. Since Ashton's diagnosis of ADHD and Autism
at four, we had done everything we could to ensure he received the support he
needed for his first official year. We expected an adjustment period, but we didn't
anticipate the relentless phone calls.

At some points, it was daily. Some were about Ashton having a meltdown, hiding
under a table, or refusing to do his work. Other calls were positive or related to
all four of our children. But for me, every time I saw the school's number pop
up on my phone, my body went into flight mode. My heart raced, my stomach
tightened, and my mind scrambled for an escape. Anything to avoid hearing what
I was sure would be another complaint about my son, which would trigger my
frustration and push me into advocacy mode.

I started screening calls, putting my phone on silent, making excuses for why I
couldn't answer. Even when the call wasn't about Ashton, my nervous system
had already braced for bad news. I wasn't just anxious. I was running from it.

At first, I judged myself. Why can't I just handle this better? I'm a bad mother. I
judged them too. Why am I constantly having to advocate and educate? Shouldn't
they already know this? But then I caught myself, realising these questions didn't
matter. It was about my nervous system doing what it was wired to do—protect
me from perceived threats. That's when I realised I could meet myself with grace
and compassion instead of criticism.

What I was experiencing was a sign that my nervous system was under strain. The
vagus nerve, central to how our bodies regulate and recover from stress, wasn't

getting the support it needed. Understanding this helped me shift my response. Instead of immediately answering the phone in a state of tension, I gave myself permission to pause. I listened to the voicemail first. Then, shook my hands before placing them on my heart, I took a slow breath. I hummed gently, feeling the soft vibration soothe my body. With each breath, I reminded myself that I don't have to solve everything right now, that I can meet this moment with compassion, both for Ashton and for myself.

When I called the school back, I wasn't *only* in the sympathetic state of flight anymore. There was still nervous energy moving through me, moments where I could feel myself jump between flight and steadiness. And alongside that, ventral vagal presence had come online too.

I was holding both.
Nervousness and courage.
Activation and grounding.

From that place, I could stay present, advocate for my son with clarity, and not rush myself through the conversation. Just as importantly, I showed up for myself with the same compassion I offered him. I met myself with grace.

This practice of pausing, regulating, and extending myself grace became a turning point. Each time I chose to nourish my nervous system instead of pushing through, I noticed more space, more clarity, and more capacity. I could feel myself meeting the moment differently, less braced and more present. I supported myself through the hard moments, and in doing so, I felt a deep sense of pride. By tending to my own regulation, I was able to show up for my son in the way he needed, and in the way I needed too.

Looking back now, I see how far I've come. I no longer screen the phone calls or brace for the worst. I've learnt to pause, take a deep breath with intention, nourish myself before I answer, and meet the moment with a sense of connection and courage. Through this practice, I've grown in ways I never expected, learning that offering myself grace in those challenging moments not only helped me navigate stress, but also deepened my ability to be present with my children and advocate for them from a place of clarity and compassion.

Graceful Reminder
*You are allowed to show yourself grace in every moment, especially
the hard ones. Through this presence, courage and clarity naturally
unfold.*

I Remember

In the moments when everything feels like too much. When the noise, the weight, and the uncertainty seem endless,

I choose to remember.

I remember the times I wanted to fight against the discomfort, pushing through with force, believing that if I just tried harder, I could control it. But I have learnt that strength is not in the struggle. It is in the softness, in allowing myself to meet what is here with grace.

I remember the times I wanted to run, to escape the feelings rising within me. When my heart raced and my breath grew shallow, urging me to find a way out. Now, I choose to pause and take intentional deep breaths, letting each inhale and exhale remind me that I am safe here, that I do not need to outrun what wants to be felt.

I remember the times I froze, caught in the stillness of uncertainty, unable to find the words or take the next step. But even in the quiet, something within me remains steady, waiting patiently for me to return. I let grace find me here, softening the edges of fear, gently guiding me back to myself.

I remember the times I sought to please, to make myself smaller so others would feel more comfortable. But I am learning that I do not have to shape myself to be worthy of kindness. I invite grace to surround me like a quiet embrace, to hold me in compassion,

AND TO REMIND ME THAT MY WORTH IS NOT MEASURED BY HOW WELL I FIT INTO THE EXPECTATIONS OF OTHERS.

WITH EACH BREATH, I REMEMBER TO RETURN TO MYSELF.

GROUNDED, HELD, AND WHOLE.

PART THREE

Cultivating Safety within

Building the Foundation of Safety

What does safety feel like in your body? Not just as a thought but as a felt sense in your breath, skin, and heartbeat. For many people, the answer is not clear. Safety can feel unfamiliar or even uncomfortable if your nervous system is used to being on alert. Yet it is this very sense of safety that creates the foundation for healing. It allows your body to come out of protection and into presence.

For some, the body has become a place of unrest. Even in quiet moments, there is an undercurrent of tension. The nervous system is still bracing. Feeling safe might not come naturally, especially when your body has learnt through experience that the world is unpredictable or unsafe. But over time, through gentle and consistent support, the body can begin to remember. It can learn to soften. It can feel a sense of safety.

I once worked with a client named Amy, who had spent years forgetting what it felt like to feel safe in her own body. On the surface, everything appeared fine. She was successful, had a loving family, and managed her life well. But underneath, her nervous system was stuck in the sympathetic state. Even when she tried to rest, she felt the need to keep going. Stillness felt strange and unfamiliar. Her body, though seemingly healthy, was caught in survival and that state shaped every part of her life.

In one session, Amy shared how deeply exhausted she was. She was tired of always being on alert. Her body never felt like it could fully relax. It was as though she was always waiting for something to go wrong, even if everything around her seemed fine. The very idea of feeling safe had become foreign. Her nervous system had been in a state of stress for so long that letting go felt impossible.

We began by resourcing into the body. For Amy, this meant simple practices: noticing her breath, gentle movement, and tuning into the subtle sensations that were always present but often ignored. The goal was not to fix or force anything, but to offer her body small invitations to reconnect and feel safe. At first, Amy felt resistant. Her system was used to moving fast and staying guarded. That resistance made sense. It told us her body was not yet ready to soften. But it also told us where we could begin.

Over time, these small moments of connection grew. Her nervous system started to trust the process. She noticed subtle changes in her body. There was a softening in her shoulders, a steadier breath, a sense of spaciousness in her chest. She felt a little less anxious in everyday situations and more present with her children, able to truly listen and respond rather than react. She found herself able to pause without rushing to fill the silence. Rest began to feel nourishing instead of uncomfortable. These were significant shifts. Her body remembered what it felt like to be safe. Grounded, open, and at home within herself.

Safety became the ground that allowed self-compassion to grow. Amy no longer had to work so hard to hold herself together. She could soften. She could listen. Amy could let herself be. It was as though the door to her inner world was slowly opening, and with it came a sense of grace that had always been there, waiting for her to feel ready enough to receive it.

Safety in the body supports more than just rest. It allows for emotional, mental, and spiritual restoration. It gives us access to the deeper layers of healing. It helps us return to ourselves with kindness and curiosity.

When your nervous system is stuck in survival, whether from stress, trauma, or overwhelm, it is hard to access ease or trust. Your body does not need to be convinced to relax. It needs to feel safe enough to do so. And that safety comes from within. It comes from learning to notice your body's cues, recognising what state you are in, and meeting yourself there without judgement.

We can only meet the truth when we feel safe enough to hold it. If this speaks to you, know that you are not alone, and you are not broken. Your body has been protecting you in the best way it knows how. What once helped you survive may no longer be needed now, and that awareness gently opens the door to change.

Cultivating safety is not about forcing calm. It is about reconnecting with yourself. It is about building a relationship with your body that is rooted in trust.

And from that place, healing becomes possible. You become the sanctuary your nervous system has been seeking. You become the safety you never knew you could be.

Graceful Reminder

The journey to healing starts with safety. When your nervous system feels secure, you create space for growth, connection, and embodied grace.

Exploring the Path of Safety

Many people are curious about the tangible, logical ways to know whether they've truly cultivated safety within their nervous system. It's a valid question, one that speaks to the mind's desire for clarity and certainty. After all, when the body takes the lead in healing, the mind may wonder why it should release its tight grip on control. It's doing its best to protect you, after all.

No matter what stories, beliefs, or experiences you're carrying with you, beneath all of that noise lies something far deeper. The core essence of who you truly are. At your core is the Self, your higher self, the infinite spark of the divine, God, the universe. It's always there, waiting for you to reconnect.

Dr. Richard Schwartz, the founder of Internal Family Systems, introduced the concept of the 8 Cs[2]. These qualities: Calmness, Curiosity, Clarity, Compassion, Confidence, Creativity, Courage, and Connectedness serve as signposts of the Self's presence within you. When you notice even subtle glimpses of these qualities, it signals that your nervous system is moving toward safety, grounding, and alignment.

These 8 Cs are:

Calmness: A deep sense of peace, even amidst life's challenges.

Curiosity: An open-hearted willingness to explore without judgement.

Clarity: Clear insight that cuts through the fog of confusion or doubt.

Compassion: A loving and gentle understanding of yourself and others.

Confidence: A grounded trust in your ability to navigate whatever comes your way.

Creativity: The flow of inspiration and new ideas that emerge naturally.

Courage: The strength to act in alignment with your truth, even in the face of fear.

Connectedness: The deep sense of unity with yourself, others, and the universe.

When you notice even the slightest shift toward one or more of these qualities, take a moment to recognise that you've found safety within yourself. Becoming aware of it allows your nervous system to send a powerful message to your brain, *You are safe*. And from there, you can begin to nurture and grow that sense of safety. This marks the start of creating a nervous system that feels held, secure, and free to expand into the fullness of your potential.

Practice: Embodying the 8 C's

Find a position that feels safe and comfortable, either seated or lying down. Close your eyes if it feels safe, or soften your gaze. Take a gentle breath in and exhale slowly, allowing your body to settle into the support beneath you.

Bring your awareness inward, noticing whatever sensations are present in your body. You may begin to sense one or more of the 8 Cs: Curiosity, Clarity, Confidence, Compassion, Courage, Creativity, Calm, or Connectedness.

If a quality arises, you can place your hands on the area where it is felt, breathe into that space, and allow it to expand at its own pace.

If no qualities are present, that is completely okay. There is no need to force or manufacture a sensation. You can simply offer a gentle invitation, such as silently saying, "I welcome curiosity" or "I allow compassion to exist here." Focus on intention rather than expectation. Even imagining the quality, or noticing a subtle shift in your attention, is enough to begin a connection.

Notice where this awareness appears in your body. You might sense warmth, lightness, openness, or simply a sense of noticing. Breathe into this space, letting the quality expand gently and safely. Stay present without judgement or pressure.

Take another slow, mindful breath, allowing the awareness of the 8 Cs whether fully felt or only lightly imagined to settle into your being. When you feel ready, gently carry this awareness into the rest of your day, noticing how these qualities can support your actions, thoughts, and presence in ways that feel safe and nourishing.

The Power of Glimmers

There was a day recently when I was sitting quietly beneath the Jacaranda tree in my backyard. The sunlight filtered through the purple blossoms in gentle shimmering patches. I felt the soft breeze on my skin and heard the distant laughter of my children playing. As the light danced through the blossoms, I noticed a deep breath I had not realised I was holding release slowly from my body. This was a glimmer.

Glimmers are brief moments when the body senses it is safe, an unfolding of ease that can be felt even in the midst of tension. A term coined by behavioural neuroscientist Stephen Porges[3] and reintroduced by therapist Deb Dana[4] describes cues that guide the body toward a sense of safety and connection, activating the ventral vagal state. They are the delicate counterpart to triggers, which activate the sympathetic and dorsal vagal states.

For me, these glimmers often come from simple tender experiences: the warmth of a cup of tea in my hands, the embrace of one of my four children, or the soothing sound of rain tapping on the window. These moments might seem insignificant to others, but they hold incredible power. They remind us that safety is available, even when the world feels overwhelming.

When we catch a glimmer, our bodies experience one or more of the eight Cs: Curiosity, Clarity, Confidence, Compassion, Courage, Creativity, Calm, and Connectedness. These are the whispers of Embodied Grace, invitations to soften and open.

The nervous system is always looking for signals of safety or threat. When glimmers enter our awareness, they offer cues of safety, helping us shift out of survival mode, the fight, flight, freeze, or fawn responses, and into connection and ease. Grace blooms in that space where we stop bracing and begin to flow with life's unfolding.

The beauty of glimmers is that they are always present. We simply need to tune in.

When I feel rushed or overwhelmed, I slow down and notice the small gifts around me like birds singing, sunlight on my skin, or the texture of a weighted blanket. At the end of the day, I often reflect on these moments to deepen my sense of safety and ease. I nourish grounding through warm tea, gentle music, and soft lighting. Simple moments of kindness and warmth like a smile or an embrace are precious glimmers that remind me I am not alone.

Play and creativity are also powerful invitations for the nervous system to feel safe. Dancing in my living room, even if it is just silly and imperfect, sparks joy and signals to my body that it can relax and be free.

By weaving glimmers into our daily lives, we build an inner sense of safety. It is not about avoiding stress or difficulty but about cultivating resilience to soften into the present, even in hard moments.

What I love about glimmers is how they remind us that we do not need to wait for grand changes or dramatic breakthroughs to feel safe or whole. The path to nervous system safety and embodied grace is built on these small tender moments. And the more we notice them, the more they notice us back.

Embodied Insight
Where can you notice a glimmer in your day right now?

Softening Into Safety

True safety is not something we force. It is something we soften into by meeting ourselves with gentleness and presence. When we approach our nervous system with curiosity instead of judgement, we create the conditions for healing. Softening is not ignoring discomfort but witnessing it without resistance.

Your nervous system is always communicating through the way your body feels, the rhythm of your breath, the thoughts that arise, and the emotions that surface. By tuning in with curiosity and without judgement, you can begin to discern whether you are in a ventral vagal, sympathetic, or dorsal vagal state.

Softening into safety helps your nervous system shift from survival into a state where healing and growth can occur. When your system feels safe, it can release tension, regulate stress hormones, and restore balance. This internal sense of safety creates space to be present, make clearer decisions, and connect more deeply with yourself and others.

I often notice this in moments of simple connection with my heart. No matter where I am, I place my hand over my heart and simply breathe for as long as I need. As I soften into the experience, my nervous system shifts gently. It is not because I force it, but because I give it permission to feel safe. Small moments like this remind me that the body naturally knows how to release tension when we allow it space.

When I feel safe, my body opens. My breath is steady, my mind clear, and my movements fluid. But when safety feels distant, my system contracts. My breath becomes shallow, my thoughts race or slow, and my body holds tension or numbness. Rather than trying to fix these states, I simply notice them. Awareness itself is a powerful act of self-care.

Each time you honour your body's signals with kindness, you build trust within your system. Safety is not something external to chase, but something you can cultivate within.

Some days safety may feel effortless. Other days it may seem just out of reach. That is okay. Progress is not about speed, but the gentleness you show yourself along the way. Moment by moment, breath by breath, you are not just healing. You are creating a life where you can thrive with greater ease, resilience, and connection.

Keep going. Each small step is building something beautiful within you.

Graceful Reminder
Softening is the courage to meet yourself with tenderness, allowing safety to grow from within.

Coming Home

When I was a uniformed police officer, part of my daily routine involved wearing heavy black boots for a minimum of twelve hours a shift. To protect my skin, I'd pair them with long black socks, creating a barrier against the chafing edge of the boots. By the end of the day, my feet felt weighed down, not just by the boots themselves but by the sheer intensity of the job. Taking those boots off was like shedding layers of the day. It was pure relief.

Over time, this act of removing my boots became a ritual. I'd come home, take my boots off and step into the shower, letting the water cascade over me. The water washed away the emotional and physical weight of the day. There's a profound wisdom in water, a gift from Mother Earth herself, flowing with renewal and release. It felt as though she was soothing me through her element, reminding me to let go and replenish.

After the shower, I'd leave my feet bare, allowing them to meet the surface beneath me, whether it was cool floorboards, soft carpet, the roughness of dirt, or the gentle blades of grass. I often stepped onto the grass, letting my bare feet connect with the earth.

I was communing with Mother Earth. The water had calmed me, and the earth beneath my feet completed the connection. It felt like an embrace of something greater, a nurturing presence offering love and wisdom. This simple practice did more than soothe my tired feet, it cultivated a deep sense of safety within my nervous system. It reminded me that I wasn't alone, that there was a constant source of stability and care beneath and around me.

When I became a detective, lighter shoes replaced my boots, but the ritual stayed. After every shift, I'd still come home, take that healing shower, and let my bare feet reconnect with the earth.

And then, somehow, without even noticing, I stopped.

I can't pinpoint exactly when it happened. Life got busy, juggling the demands of work, parenting, and everything else in between. The ritual faded into the background, overshadowed by the chaos of daily life. I could give myself countless reasons for why it slipped away. "I'm too busy with the kids" being a common one, but the truth was, I had lost touch with something that anchored me.

It wasn't until the pandemic that the realisation hit me. One evening, after a long shift as a detective, I came home and kicked off my shoes. Now lighter than my old black boots but somehow leaving my feet feeling even heavier. That familiar weight brought back memories of my old ritual, of the times when I'd consciously connect with the earth and water. I knew what I needed to do.

That evening, I stepped into the shower, letting the water cleanse me as it once had, and then stepped outside, barefoot. The cool grass met my feet like an old friend, and at that moment, I reconnected with the love, light, and wisdom of Mother Earth. Through her water and her land, she welcomed me back as if no time had passed. It was as though she whispered, "Welcome home."

Embodied Insight

Where do you feel most grounded and supported? Reflect on a place either in nature or within yourself that brings you softness. How can you carry that feeling into your daily life?

Expansion Through Small Steps

Healing and growth unfold through small grace filled steps. Each time you offer yourself grace, a soft breath, a moment of stillness, or a gentle word instead of criticism, you are taking a step toward safety and connection. These are simple, intentional actions that tell your body and nervous system, "You are safe. You are supported." Over time, they create the foundation from which true expansion becomes possible.

Small steps might look like placing a hand over your heart, noticing your breath, pausing to feel your feet on the ground, or simply giving yourself permission to rest. They might also be trying something new, choosing to meet frustration with kindness, or allowing emotions to move through you without judgement. Each moment of grace teaches your nervous system that it is safe to relax, process, and connect. Safety within the body is the soil in which growth can take root.

Expansion happens when the nervous system feels secure enough to explore. These small acts of grace build trust in your body and cultivate resilience, allowing you to meet tension, restlessness, or discomfort with curiosity instead of resistance. From this grounded place, emotions like grief, anger, or shame become invitations to grow rather than obstacles to overcome.

Consistent attention to these small steps helps you flow between challenge and rest, activation and ease, uncertainty and possibility. From a regulated state of safety, you can stretch beyond comfort zones, explore new emotional landscapes, deepen connections, and embrace life fully.

Each small act of grace is a practice of embodied living. It reminds you that healing and expansion are not distant destinations but living experiences available in every breath, every choice, and every heartbeat. Moment by moment, breath by breath, you are nurturing safety, cultivating resilience, and opening yourself to a life of connection, compassion, and Embodied Grace.

Graceful Reminder
Every small step you take is an act of grace. Each breath, each choice, each gentle gesture teaches your body and heart that you are safe, worthy, and capable of expansion.

Listening at Last

It was at the end of another long, gruelling shift as a frontline detective that it hit me. I had been moving through life on autopilot for what felt like forever. Answering calls, writing reports, managing multiple cases, preparing for trials. At home things felt no lighter. My kids were always the first to be dropped off at daycare and the last to be picked up. Most days were filled with therapies, appointments, and logistics. My husband and I were like two ships passing in the night, each of us trying to keep everything afloat: the bills, the kids, the endless lists in between.

The strain was relentless, and I could feel myself drowning. The weight sat heavy in my chest, the tension gripped my neck, and fatigue seeped into every part of me. I had been numbing myself with food and alcohol, gaining weight while stuck in fight or flight, surviving rather than living.

I had always prided myself on being strong and in control. But one night, sitting in my car after overtime, I realised I was on the brink of burnout. Somewhere along the way, I had lost myself. I wasn't living, only getting by. That moment of clarity became my wake-up call, a threshold into listening at last. I had been solving everyone else's problems while ignoring my own. I was numb and disconnected, yet something inside me longed for more.

I knew I needed to create a safer space within, a place to rest and reconnect with who I really was. I did not know where to begin, only that I had to start. The first step was honesty. I was carrying too much: part-time work with a full-time caseload, four children, the household, the invisible load that never stopped. My body had been whispering for years, but I kept pushing through. Until it was no longer a whisper. It was loud and undeniable. I was breaking. And in that breaking I discovered that true strength was not holding it all together, but letting myself fall apart.

I started small. I breathed. Not the shallow, anxious breaths I was used to, but slow, intentional ones, one hand on my heart and one on my belly, feeling myself arrive again. It was not a quick fix, but it was a beginning. I walked in nature and let the earth hold what I had been carrying.

When anger rose, I stopped trying to swallow it. I felt the heat in my chest, the tightness in my jaw, the urge to clench and push through. Instead of judging it, I let it move. Sometimes that meant shaking my arms out in the kitchen when no one was watching. Sometimes it meant crying in the shower. Sometimes it meant stepping outside and letting my voice rise, not in harm, not at anyone, but as sound. A contained release. A safe expression of what had been held in for too long. Sometimes it meant pressing my feet firmly into the ground and letting my body discharge what it had carried for years.

I learned to let the anger move through my throat instead of trapping it in my chest. I learned that sound could be medicine when it was conscious. I reached out for support from a somatic practitioner and allowed myself to not do it all alone. I attuned to my body and began listening differently.

The anger was not wrong. It was protective. Beneath it was grief. Beneath the grief was exhaustion.

Slowly, as I stopped fighting what I felt, safety began to return.

And as I stopped fighting what I felt, something unexpected happened. The anger softened. Not because it disappeared, but because it was finally heard. Beneath the intensity was a longing to be supported, to be met, to not have to carry everything alone.

The shift came when I realised that creating inner safety was about showing up for myself, not doing everything perfectly. It was not about never feeling stress again, but about meeting those feelings with compassion. It was about building resilience, listening to what my nervous system was saying, and supporting it with the tools I was learning.

As I grew safer within, my capacity expanded. I could hold more, without being consumed. I stopped relying on circumstances to dictate my state and began showing up more fully: for the victims I served, my colleagues, and my children.

The more grounded I became, the more I could be myself. I no longer needed a mask. The peace I found within became an anchor, something I could return to whenever life felt overwhelming.

Looking back, that was the turning point. The moment I shifted from surviving to truly living. I realised I did not need to burn out to be effective. I could balance the demands of my work with the peace I longed for. That inner space of safety became the foundation of my healing, leading me toward the grace I had been seeking all along.

True power, I now believe, is not in enduring the storm, but in learning to stand steady and at peace within, no matter what comes.

Graceful Reminder
Your nervous system doesn't need more pressure; it needs permission to soften, to slow, to feel safe.

The Body That Holds Me

For much of my life, my relationship with my body was complicated. I felt I had to control it, push it, or fix it. I ignored its signals of fatigue, tension, and hunger, pushing through discomfort to meet the demands of work and life. When I overate or binged, harsh self-criticism followed. My body felt like something to battle rather than a guide or companion.

I remember the tightness in my chest after a binge, the knot in my stomach, the ache of tension and shame. I pushed through or retreated into numbness. Slowly, I began to notice these sensations as messages—invitations to slow down and care for myself. The goal was no longer to silence discomfort, but to meet my body with enough support that it could soften in its own time. Healing began when I stopped working against my body and started listening.

Much of my tension came from a desire to control, shaped by internalised narratives that I was not enough. I see now that my body was never the problem. It was trying to protect and guide me, carrying my stories, my trauma, and even the joy I had neglected. When I began to truly listen, I started to understand myself in ways I never had before.

Releasing control and embracing compassion changed everything. My body became a sanctuary where I could rest and reconnect. It wasn't about loving every part immediately, but about approaching my body with curiosity, kindness, and patience, allowing its wisdom to support me.

Listening revealed buried emotions—grief beneath anger, shame and guilt held for years. Meeting these sensations with compassion uncovered needs and wisdom I had carried all along. Small acts of care reshaped my relationship with my body, turning it from adversary into ally.

Now, my body feels like a companion. When I move with care, breathe deeply, and honour its signals, I feel its strength and softness. It is the vessel through which I experience life and healing, each sensation a doorway that grounds me and reminds me I am always held.

Practice: Grateful Body Scan

Find a comfortable seated or lying position where you will not be disturbed. Close your eyes if that feels safe, or soften your gaze to a fixed point. Take a few deep breaths, releasing tension with each exhale and allowing your body to settle into the present moment.

Bring your attention to your feet and legs, noticing any sensations and silently thanking them for supporting you. Move your awareness to your hips, lower back, and abdomen, acknowledging their strength and nourishment.

Shift your focus to your heart, lungs, arms, hands, shoulders, and neck. Feel your breath and heartbeat, noticing any sensations, and offer gratitude for their care and support.

Now, bring attention to your face, jaw, eyes, mouth, and mind. Thank them for all that they do each day.

Finally, sense your body as a whole, appreciating its interconnectedness and its role as your trusted ally. Ask yourself, "Which part feels most held, and what does it invite me to feel or do next?"

Take a few more deep breaths, letting this sense of gratitude and presence settle within you before gently opening your eyes and returning to the room.

Beyond Time and Space

Our nervous system responds beyond the usual boundaries of past, present, and future. It can react to memories or anticipations as if they are happening now. This unique aspect of our physiology can be a beautiful gift, especially when we learn to use it to create and cultivate safety and connection within ourselves.

What if safety could arise inside you right now? Not something you have to wait for or find outside yourself, but something that grows from within, in this very moment. This is not only possible, it is a natural part of who you are. As Richard Schwartz[5] teaches in Internal Family Systems, we all carry parts that need safety and compassion. By tuning in to these parts and the subtle sensations of our body, we create space for inner safety to emerge. You might notice the softening of your breath, the gentle glimmer of grace, or even the presence of one or more of the 8 Cs: Compassion, Curiosity, Clarity, Connection, Courage, Calm, Confidence, and Creativity.

After practising for some time, I have become more attuned to the subtle cues my nervous system and body display. I can now easily notice where there is a sense of ease in my body, even if it is just a faint glimmer. When I place my hand gently on my chest, I feel a softening in my heart, an invitation from my body to pause and be present. This small, intentional gesture creates a ripple of safety that expands throughout my body, gently shifting my nervous system from a state of anxiousness to one of grounded calm.

Memories are a wonderful way to cultivate safety within. A client of mine often took herself back to a peaceful beach vacation to invite a sense of connection. She recalled the gentle sound of waves crashing, the feeling of warm sand beneath her feet and the expansive horizon. By bringing these memories into focus, she activated the 8 Cs, especially connection and clarity, allowing her nervous system to relax and feel more regulated.

If memories feel out of reach or too distant, we can also imagine a place where safety, connection and peace could arise. This might be a mountaintop, a forest, a quiet garden or even a favourite chair. By gently turning our attention to these places, we invite safety and groundedness into the body, creating a sense of calm that moves beyond time and space.

The beauty of this practice is that it does not require changing the outside world. Instead, we learn to access the safety already within us, no matter what is happening around us. Through these practices, we discover the power to nurture and support our nervous system in ways that feel deeply healing and empowering.

By tuning into softening sensations, drawing from memories or using our imagination gently, we weave through safety within the layers of our being. In doing so, we give ourselves the gift of peace, groundedness and healing, no matter where we are or what we are facing.

Practice: Embodied Connection

Find a comfortable seated or lying position. Close your eyes if that feels safe, or soften your gaze. Take a deep breath in through your nose, welcoming light and compassion, and exhale slowly through your mouth. Let your body soften, releasing tension and grounding into the present moment.

Bring to mind a place that feels safe, peaceful, or comforting. It might be a memory, an imagined space, or somewhere you feel drawn to. Notice the feelings it evokes in your body. Ask yourself, "Where do I feel this sense of connection?" Observe without judgement.

Pay attention to the sensations that arise. Perhaps warmth, lightness, soft pressure, or gentle pulsing. It might be subtle or strong. Allow curiosity to guide you, noticing the quality, location, and movement of the feeling.

If it feels possible, place your hand on that area. If not, place your hand on your heart. Let your breath flow into that space, expanding the sensation with each inhale and softening tension with each exhale. Imagine the feeling spreading through your body, filling you with grounding, safety, and calm.

Stay with the sensation for a few breaths, allowing it to grow and deepen. There is no right or wrong way to feel this. Simply notice and expand it naturally.

When you are ready, gently remove your hand and bring your awareness back to the room. Trust that this place of connection is always within you. You can return to it whenever you need safety, grounding, or calm.

Rooted in Grace

Embodied Grace deepens when we ground our nervous system in safety, resilience, and self-compassion. To be rooted in grace is to trust our own unfolding, to stand in our truth even when uncertainty arises, and to recognise grace as a foundation we can return to again and again.

For a long time I believed resilience meant pushing through, standing tall no matter what. I had been conditioned to equate strength with endurance, with suppressing, ignoring, and surviving. But over time I discovered that true resilience does not come from rigidity. It comes from the nervous system. From feeling safe enough to soften. From the ability to regulate after stress and to adapt without becoming stuck in survival. A resilient nervous system is flexible and responsive, not hardened.

In my past as a detective, I avoided, dissociated, and compartmentalised emotions to survive. I responded to external chaos while silencing my inner world. My breath was shallow, my body tight, and I thought I was strong. But in truth, I was disconnected.

Only through somatic healing did I begin to feel safe within myself again. The first time I truly listened to my body, I noticed tension, a racing heart, and held breath. Rather than ignoring it, I paid attention. I placed a hand on my heart, closed my eyes, and allowed myself to feel.

That moment planted a seed. What if I could nourish my nervous system instead of dismissing it?

Self-regulation became my path forward. Breathing deeply. Grounding. Tapping. Moving. Shaking to release old patterns. I began to rewire my nervous system. Slowly, my body started to trust me again.

Regulation is not about perfection. It is about returning. Again and again.

And we do not do it alone. Our nervous systems are wired for connection. Healing happens not just within us but between us. When we sit with someone who is grounded, when we are met with compassion, our body exhales. We regulate through connection with safe, attuned people.

Many of my clients believed they had to heal alone. But as they allowed connection through co-regulation and meaningful support, they realised healing deepened in relationship.

When we create safety within and around us, we open to more than just surviving. We begin to expand.

Expansion is possible when our nervous system feels supported enough to move beyond survival. When we are no longer bracing, we start expressing, dreaming, and creating. We let go of what no longer serves not as a loss but as wisdom. We honour the seasons of our healing.

Living in survival, I believed expansion was for someone else. Someone with less trauma or a calmer past. But healing is not about erasing history. It is about integrating it.

As I found safety, I began to expand. I let myself soften. I allowed myself to dream and create. I realised I was never meant to endure forever. I was meant to rise.

By tending to our nervous system through awareness, self-regulation, and co-regulation, we create the foundation for true expansion. Growth begins within.

As a recovering perfectionist, I will remind you often that embodied grace is not about doing it all right. It is about trusting your nervous system's ability to return. It is about deepening into wholeness.

So I invite you to reflect. Are you tending to your nervous system or ignoring its signals? Are you offering it nourishment or leaving it in depletion? Are you trusting your own expansion?

Because when you truly root into awareness, regulation, and connection, you do not just survive. You thrive. You rise. You embody grace in its most expansive form.

And that is a life worth living.

Embodied Insight
How are you currently nourishing your nervous system so it feels supported enough to expand beyond survival?

PART FOUR

Intuitive Intelligence

Already Held

Grace doesn't come only after the pain has passed. It moves with us through the ache, the breaking open, and the moments we cannot yet name. It sits beside us when there are no words, no clear answers, only the guidance of something deeper asking us to trust. Grace carries us through both the falling apart and the return to wholeness.

In that presence, I have come to understand that grace is what helps us breathe through it, and from that same stillness, Intuitive Intelligence® arises. It is the knowing beneath thought, the felt sense in the body, the images that appear, and the sounds and signs that guide us when reason falls silent. While the full depth of Intuitive Intelligence® will unfold in the chapters ahead, even now, when we soften enough to listen, Embodied Grace and Intuitive Intelligence® are already there, holding us in the dark and guiding us home.

When Grant and I were trying for our third child, there was a hope in my heart, a picture of what it might be like to welcome another baby and complete our family. Grant and I had our own timeline, our own rhythm for how it would unfold. Each month, I would quietly slip into the bathroom to take a pregnancy test, waiting for a positive result. But again and again, month after month, only a negative result appeared. It felt like a repeated stab in my womb. I tried not to hold on too tightly, but disappointment settled in.

And then came the physical pain.

I injured my back, and something shifted in a way I could not reverse. What began as a strain became something much deeper. I was in agony. I could not move without wincing. I cried at night. I screamed into pillows. The pain took over my life. I was exhausted, not just from the injury, but from how relentless it was. Nothing helped. I lay in bed with painkillers that dulled my senses but never reached the root of what I was feeling.

Specialist after specialist told me that now was not the time to fall pregnant. One, with firmness, told me I should not have another child at all, that my back simply would not cope with another pregnancy. His words pierced deeper than he knew. He was not just speaking about my spine, he was telling me that the life I longed for might no longer be possible.

I felt broken.

Not just physically. There was a sorrow that sat heavy on my chest, like something sacred was slipping away and I could not catch it. I was already a mother, but something in me longed to birth again. That trust was shaking. I felt raw, tender, and very alone.

One day, I could not bear to be inside anymore. I felt a little nudge, a pull I did not want to follow because my body was in so much pain that even stepping outside felt like an operation. And yet, something beneath the discomfort insisted. I hobbled into the bushland near our home, relieved to be somewhere that was not sterile or clinical, beyond the lounge, the bed, or the quiet walls of my home. I needed air and space for my pain to breathe. Up until this point, I had been trying to numb through the pain, to solve it, and to force an answer. I was gripping so tightly to the outcome that I couldn't hear what was already whispering underneath.

I stood barefoot on the earth, surrounded by trees that had lived far longer than I had. The sky was overcast, the light soft and muted. The ground smelled of soil and eucalyptus. There was no breeze. Everything was still.

And then something happened that I did not expect. In the silence, something inside me softened. I was still hurting. I was still grieving. But the rawness made room for something else, a voice. Not outside me, not booming from the sky, but a voice of certainty deep in my body. Not thought, not logic, just knowing.

It said, "Be patient. You will get pregnant."

The voice was not demanding. It was not full of promise. It did not rise with excitement. It was calm. Grounded. It felt like it belonged to the earth itself. It came with no timeline, no plan, only presence. At the time, I didn't know to call it Intuitive Intelligence®. I only knew it felt real, rooted, and undeniable. But looking back, I see it now for what it was—my body, my soul, and God speaking as one.

I stood there for a long time, letting the trees hold my pain, letting the silence wrap around me. I did not feel fixed, but I did feel held.

In the months that followed, the tests remained negative. Still, I remembered the voice. I remembered how it felt in my body. I stopped reaching so hard and I began to let go. Not of the dream, but of the timeline. The circumstances hadn't changed, but I had. That knowing, that embodied certainty, didn't give me a roadmap. It gave me a rhythm. A steadiness that allowed me to wait without collapsing.

Then one day, the pregnancy test came back positive.

But even then, it was not simple. My blood tests showed very low levels of human chorionic gonadotropin, known as HCG, a hormone that supports pregnancy. The doctor told me that my levels were too low for a viable pregnancy and that I should prepare for a miscarriage. I was to return in a week for another blood test and was told to expect bleeding. Normally, I would have panicked. I would have paced the house, cried in the shower, bracing for the moment I would see the first streak of blood. That kind of waiting is its own kind of pain. But something in me was different this time. I remembered the bushland. I remembered that voice. And I knew, even with the numbers and the odds, that this pregnancy would hold.

And it did.

Not only did it hold, but it became two. Twins. A double gift. A double unfolding. The grace that met me in the bushland was not a reward for faith or a miracle I earned. It was the truth that I had always been held, even in my most broken moment. I just needed stillness to hear it.

That is when I truly began to understand Intuitive Intelligence®. It is not about receiving the answers we want. It is about being open enough to hear the truth that already lives inside us. Intuitive Intelligence® is not just instinct. It is not a gut feeling or an emotional reaction. It is deeper, more spacious and grounded. It is the wisdom that emerges when we soften, when we are present enough to feel what is real beneath the noise.

And grace, she arrives right there. Not to fix, but to hold.

Intuitive Intelligence® and grace rise together. Both offer guidance and surrender. Both show us the way and give us the strength to walk it. Intuitive Intelligence® does not always make the path easier, but grace reminds us we never have to walk it alone.

Following intuition alone does not always mean we are acting with spiritual wisdom. At times, what we perceive as intuition is actually a reactive part of us speaking, a desire, a fear, or an impulse shaped by conditioning and past experience. These inner echoes can cloud our ability to hear true guidance.

There will be moments when the knowing in your body is strong, but your mind is full of doubt. You will wonder if you are being foolish. You will worry that you are making it up.

And that is when grace meets you again. She does not ask you to be certain. She simply reminds you that you are already held.

Perhaps you've had a moment like this too, where the world went quiet just long enough for truth to rise. You may not have called it intuition or Intuitive Intelligence®, but something in you recognised its tone. Even if it was fleeting. Even if you doubted it later. That is the beginning of your own remembering.

Let Intuitive Intelligence® and grace walk with you in the waiting, in the unravelling, in the moments of stillness and the moments of clarity. They move with you, steady and present, guiding you to trust your own knowing.

Embodied Insight
Where in your life do you feel called to practice surrender with more courage and tenderness?

The Sacred Partnership

To walk the path of Embodied Grace we must live from our Intuitive Intelligence®. It is more than a moment of insight or a gut feeling. It is a way of being a living, breathing connection with the sacred wisdom that moves through us. When our body softens, our breath deepens, and our inner knowing settles into our bones, grace begins to flow. And in those moments, we remember something ancient and comforting. We are held completely and unconditionally by God.

Grace and Intuitive Intelligence® are not separate forces. They move together in sacred partnership. Both invite us into surrender, softening us into acceptance, opening the heart with compassion, grounding us in trust, and anchoring the soul in discernment. Together, they shape a way of being that is both deeply attuned and courageously honest. When we live from this place within, we are softened by presence, guided by wisdom, and carried by something greater than ourselves.

While intuition offers us glimpses of truth, Intuitive Intelligence® teaches us how to recognise, trust, and live that truth from the inside out. Here is the difference between the two:

Intuition
Intuition is innate within us all. It is not a special gift reserved for a few. It is biological, a natural way your body, soul, and subconscious communicate with you. It speaks through sensations, symbols, and spontaneous knowing that often bypass logic. You might feel it as a nudge in the body, a tingling in your belly, a whisper in your thoughts, or a certainty that needs no explanation. Everyone is intuitive.

I remember the nudge that drew me into the bushland. My body was in pain, every step a struggle, and yet something beneath the discomfort insisted. That pull, that insistence to step outside, was intuition in action. It did not come with instructions, promises, or urgency. It simply guided me, subtly, toward what I needed.

Intuition is sacred, yet it benefits from being anchored in something deeper. This is where Intuitive Intelligence® comes in, offering presence, discernment, and a grounded path for our inner knowing to flow more freely.

Intuitive Intelligence

Intuitive Intelligence® is a deep and integrated knowing that comes from trusting and living in harmony with our intuition. It helps us move beyond fear and step into a partnership with God. Rather than being impulsive or driven by strong emotions, Intuitive Intelligence® grows from stillness, presence, and self-awareness. It is a felt sense of alignment that connects every part of who we are in mind, body, and spirit and is supported by nervous system regulation and spiritual discernment.

Founder of the Institute for Intuitive Intelligence®, my teacher and dear friend, Dr Ricci-Jane Adams describes Intuitive Intelligence® as[6]:

> *"An embodied state of being that is*
> *non-local, acausal, active, participatory,*
> *deep, creative, and surrendered."*

Though I will explore the idea of non-local intuition further in the chapters ahead, this description invites us to lean into the true nature of Intuitive Intelligence®. It is not born from logic or step-by-step reasoning. Instead, it flows from a place both within and beyond us, a knowing that transcends time and space.

It is *acausal*, meaning it does not rely on cause and effect. Sometimes, we simply sense something as true without needing to understand how or why.
It is *active and participatory*, a living, breathing energy that invites us to engage, respond, and move in harmony with its rhythm.
It is *deep and creative*, drawing from an infinite well of ancient wisdom and fresh possibilities.

And it is *surrendered,* never forced or controlled, but welcomed with openness and trust.

The moment in the bushland was more than a personal experience. It was a glimpse into something universal. That embodied knowing is what Intuitive Intelligence® feels like for me. It is not limited to extraordinary circumstances. It is a natural part of being alive, always available to guide us when we soften enough to listen. What I experienced in my body and in the stillness of the trees is one expression of the inner knowing that arises in many ways, sometimes as a nudge, sometimes as an undeniable certainty, or in ways that cannot easily be named.

In the months that followed that bushland moment, the intuitive wisdom I received that day stayed within me. I remembered how it felt in my body. Even when the tests were negative, even when the doctor told me to prepare for loss, I returned to that feeling. I didn't force belief. I didn't grip tightly. I simply stayed with what I knew deep in my bones. That was Intuitive Intelligence®. A devotion to presence, to the truth within, even when my mind wanted to doubt.

To offer a clear and grounded way of understanding this, Dr Ricci-Jane Adams shares a powerful formula for Intuitive Intelligence®[7]:

Innate Intuition + Spiritual Fierceness = Intuitive Intelligence

This formula gave me a language for something I had always felt but struggled to name. Your intuition is already within you, an ancient, wise, inner compass. But it needs to be partnered with something courageous and committed to truly flourish.

That something is spiritual fierceness. The willingness to meet your truth, even when it's uncomfortable. The daily devotion to choose presence over avoidance, love over fear, and alignment over approval. It's not always gentle. Sometimes spiritual fierceness arrives as quiet devotion, and other times it roars through you as bold action or unshakable resolve. Whether soft or intense, it's about showing up fully, even when you feel unsure, and choosing your truth again and again. This kind of devotion brings your intuitive wisdom to life. It transforms instinct into embodied knowing. It turns whispers into clarity.

Intuitive Intelligence® helps us distinguish true inner guidance from conditioned responses. It's not only about receiving insights but knowing how to live them. It requires practice, trust, patience, and a relationship with the self that is honest and tender. Living with Intuitive Intelligence® is a spiritual practice, one that may not always offer certainty, but always invites us to move with integrity.

As I trust my Intuitive Intelligence®, it rises, steady, certain, and undeniable. For me, it stays firm yet compassionate no matter what tone it takes. Each response is met with grace, present all along, simply unfolding as I arrive. When I feel lost, it moves through me like breath, soft and unseen, saying, *"You are held. Even here. Especially here."* I don't need to figure it all out. I just need to listen, soften, and stay.

Intuitive Intelligence® is a dance between the felt experience of our body and a wider field of knowing. It invites us to soften, release the need for control and certainty, and listen with our whole being. The more we allow this flow, the more it becomes a supportive companion on our journey.

This is not something we master once and for all. It is a relationship we cultivate, a sacred practice we return to again and again. It deepens as we soften. It grows stronger as we trust. And grace walks beside it, reminding us we are never truly alone as we listen for the truth within.

Graceful Reminder

When we live from Intuitive Intelligence®, we embody the infinite, where every possibility is within our reach and magnificence is our true nature.

Body and Beyond

Many describe intuition as a gut feeling, a sudden knowing that appears without logical explanation. After nearly twenty years as a police officer, I heard the phrase "gut instinct" more times than I can count. Victims would often tell me they just knew something wasn't right. Community members would reach out for help, guided only by a feeling they couldn't quite name. And officers, myself included, would walk into uncertain situations where our bodies sensed what our minds hadn't yet caught up to.

This kind of instinct is real and powerful. It is primal, protective, and rooted in our evolution, a biological gift designed to keep us safe. But it is only one expression of intuition.

Intuition is more than instinct. It is a soulful knowing that moves beyond survival. It speaks in nudges, felt sensations, emotions, inner images, and the gentle rhythms of the heart. Sometimes it arrives softly. Other times, it may feel loud or insistent to get your attention. However, your intuition communicates with you, when you learn to listen and follow it, this deeper intelligence can rise and guide you, not only in moments of danger, but also in love, purpose, healing, and expansion.

Intuition is not a rare gift reserved for a select few. It is innate and essential, part of the very fabric of your being. It belongs to everyone. It is your birthright. This inner knowing often arises before thought, grounding your decisions in something deeper than logic alone and opening the way to a more connected, expansive way of living and understanding the world.

There are many intuition teachers and thought-leaders who explore and name different kinds of intuition, each offering their own unique lens. While their frameworks and language may differ, many point to two overarching expressions of intuitive awareness: local and non-local intuition. These are not rigid categories, but rather ways to understand how intuition communicates with us, from the wisdom of the body to the vast field of the unseen.

Local Intuition: The Wisdom of the Body

How many times have you entered a room and instantly felt that something was off, even though everything looked fine? Maybe the air feels heavier than usual, or the energy subtly shifts around you. Perhaps someone's voice is slightly too high, their movements too rigid, or a stillness in the room makes your stomach tighten. That knowing, that sense beneath the surface, is local intuition speaking. It isn't thought or deduction.

I encountered this feeling countless times, both as a police officer and in daily life. Sometimes it was a tug in my chest that told me to pause or look closer. Other times it was more insistent, a rising tension in my gut that demanded I pay attention. In each moment, I learnt to trust that internal signal, even when there was no immediate evidence to justify it. That subtle awareness often kept people safe, helped prevent harm, and guided me to respond with clarity and care.

What I was experiencing in those moments is local intuition: a grounded, embodied knowing that arises from within, through our nervous system, energy field, and the subtle cues we pick up without even realising. This is where gut instinct, energetic sensitivity, and implicit knowledge live. It often speaks before our conscious mind has time to catch up.

As electromagnetic beings, we are always in silent conversation with the world around us. This is why we can sense someone's presence, feel shifts in energy, or intuitively know the mood of a room before a single word is spoken. Your energy field is receiving subtle information and translating it into a felt experience.

Scientific research supports this phenomenon. The HeartMath® Institute has found that the heart is the most powerful source of electromagnetic energy in the human body, producing the largest rhythmic electromagnetic field of any organ. This field can be detected up to three feet away and is involved in energetic communication, referred to as cardio electromagnetic communication.[8]

Additionally, studies on nonverbal communication[9] highlight the significant role of the nervous system in conveying emotions and intentions without words. The brain, spinal cord, and peripheral nerves control body movements that often communicate more than verbal language.

These findings suggest that our bodies are constantly interacting with and responding to the subtle energies and cues of those around us, reinforcing that intuition is not just a mental process but a holistic, embodied experience.

Non-Local Intuition: The Wisdom of the Universe

Intuition does not stop at what we can feel in our immediate body and environment. It also stretches beyond time, beyond space, and into realms where logic cannot follow. This is non-local intuition, a more expansive form of knowing that connects us to the infinite field of universal intelligence.

Remember those moments when you suddenly think of someone, and then receive a text message from them moments later? Or when you wake in the night with an unshakeable feeling, only to later learn a loved one across the world was in distress? That is non-local intuition in motion. It is not bound by proximity or cause and effect. It is our Intuitive Intelligence® guiding us in ways that do not always make sense to the logical mind, but that are deeply real.

Intuitive Intelligence® is the embodied expression of this deeper intuition. It helps us not only receive wisdom but live it with discernment and grace. Going forward, I may use the words *intuition* and *Intuitive Intelligence*® interchangeably. When I speak of intuition, I mean it in its fullest sense, intuition that is attuned, embodied, and guided by grace.

Institutions like the HeartMath® Institute explore this level of intuitive connection as part of the greater interconnectedness of life. We are part of a vast energetic web where thoughts, feelings, and intentions ripple across space and time.[10]

This is why we can feel the impact of a prayer, a blessing, or someone's silent well-wishes. It is why healing can be felt across distance, and why deep intuitive insight can arrive without any logical source.

When we learn to slow down, to listen deeply, and to trust what arises within, we strengthen our relationship with both forms of intuition. We remember that we are never truly alone, that guidance is always available, and that grace is always reaching for us.

Embodied Insight

Take a moment to reflect on two experiences of intuition in your life: one that felt local and one that felt non-local. For each experience consider; What guided you towards the decision or action? How did it feel to trust that inner knowing, especially if it didn't make sense at the time? What did the experience teach you about the relationship between grace, intuition, and timing in your life?

The Clairs

Have you ever wondered how your intuition communicates to you? Maybe you receive sudden insights, feel emotions deeply, hear an inner voice, or experience vivid mental images. Intuition communicates in many ways. While everyone has access to multiple intuitive channels, collectively known as the 'Clairs,' one often feels more natural, fluid, or prominent. This is known as your dominant clair.

Understanding your dominant clair can offer profound insights into how you intuitively connect with the world around you. Let's explore each clair:

Clairvoyance (Clear Seeing)

Clairvoyance is often the first thing people think of when they hear the word 'psychic,' but it's just one piece of the intuitive puzzle. Being clairvoyant means receiving intuitive information through visual impressions, which often appear as symbolic images, scenes, or colours in your mind's eye rather than literal visions. It's like watching a mental movie or seeing a flash of an image that conveys meaning.

Clairaudience (Clear Hearing)

Clairaudience allows you to receive intuitive guidance through sound. This might manifest as hearing a word, phrase, or melody in your mind, often in your own internal voice or occasionally as an external sound. It's like having a whisper of insight that directs you.

Clairsentience (Clear Feeling)

Clairsentience is the ability to intuitively feel energy, emotions, or sensations in your body. It goes beyond being an empath. It involves physical sensations like tingling, warmth, or even a sense of heaviness, which communicate messages from your intuition.

Claircognisance (Clear Knowing)

Claircognisance is the ability to simply 'know' something without prior thought, reasoning, or evidence. It feels as if a fully formed piece of information drops into your awareness out of nowhere, with undeniable certainty.

This clair is often dismissed or doubted because it can feel like your own thoughts, but the clarity and immediacy of the insight set it apart. For example, you might just 'know' that someone is about to call you or that a particular choice is the right one, even without logical reasoning to back it up.

In my first book, *The Intuitive Detective*, I shared that my dominant clair is claircognisance (clear knowing), followed by clairsentience (clear feeling), clairaudience (clear hearing), and clairvoyance (clear seeing), often appearing afterwards. As the years have passed, and I've continued to practice and strengthen my intuition, it now feels as though all the clairs come through simultaneously. However, if I break it down, claircognisance always arrives first, in that split second before the others. I describe this knowing as a voice, not because it speaks aloud, but because that's how it moves through me: immediate, clear, and undeniable.

Intuition is like a muscle that needs to be practised to grow stronger. The more you engage with your intuitive channels, listen, and follow your inner guidance, the more accessible and refined it becomes, allowing you to translate it more clearly and receive higher frequencies. Each time you trust and act on your insights, you strengthen your ability to trust yourself, building confidence and deepening your connection with your inner wisdom.

As you continue to develop this connection, understanding and honouring your dominant clair is key. Whether it's claircognisance, clairsentience, clairaudience, or clairvoyance, each represents a unique way your intuition communicates. Recognising which clair resonates most strongly within you deepens your relationship with your intuition, turning it into a reliable compass for your journey.

As you embody grace, trusting your intuition becomes more natural. This trust grows from your relationship with yourself, not from following rules. Each moment is an opportunity to check in with your intuition: What do I sense? What feels right in this moment? By attuning to your unique intuitive channels, you empower yourself to make decisions that align with your true self.

This path is one of integration and growth. As you cultivate a compassionate relationship with yourself and deepen your connection with your intuition, you unlock opportunities for transformation. Intuition isn't here to make us comfortable. It's here to guide us toward alignment with our true purpose, even if it means stepping into discomfort or the unknown. Growth often comes when we move outside our comfort zones, and intuition is your guide, lighting the way.

By following your intuition and embracing your inner guidance, you step into a life aligned with your authentic self, filled with joy, fulfilment, and grace. Though intuition may challenge you, it's always leading you toward your highest potential.

Trusting your intuition isn't just about making choices, it's about honouring yourself and the wisdom within you. As you embrace this practice, life becomes a fluid, harmonious experience, supported by the guidance of your Intuitive Intelligence®. By integrating this wisdom into your daily life, you enhance your own wellbeing and inspire others to do the same.

Practice: Awareness to Your Dominant Clair

Find a comfortable seated position. Close your eyes if that feels safe, or soften your gaze. Allow your body to settle and your mind to rest in the present moment.

Take a few deep, grounding breaths. Inhale fully through your nose, and exhale slowly through your mouth, releasing tension or stress. With each breath, feel more present and connected to yourself.

Place one hand over the centre of your chest. Feel the warmth of your hand and the rhythm of your heartbeat. Let your body soften into this touch and feel your heart's energy supporting you.

With each inhale, invite love, peace, and guidance into your heart. With each exhale, release anything that feels heavy or distracting. Spend a few minutes allowing your awareness to rest fully in your heart space.

Silently ask, "What would you have me know at this time?"

Trust that your intuition will respond. Notice how it comes through your body and mind as sensations, feelings, images, sounds, or knowing. There is no right or wrong way to receive this guidance. Simply be open and allow it to arise.

Gently scan your body and notice any subtle shifts in energy, tingling, warmth, or clarity. These sensations are your intuition speaking. Honour whatever arises without judgement.

When a response comes, acknowledge it silently. Trust that this guidance is valid and meaningful for this moment.

Before fully returning your awareness to the room, take a moment to notice how your intuition first communicated. Did it appear as a bodily sensation, a thought, an image, a sound, or an inner knowing? Simply observe without judgement. This can help you recognise your dominant intuitive sense and how you naturally receive guidance.

Take a few deeper breaths and bring your hands back to your heart centre. Hold a moment of gratitude for the wisdom and guidance you receive. Gently invite movement back into your body. Stretch or shift as needed, and when you feel ready, slowly open your eyes. Notice how your body feels now and carry this sense of connection and clarity with you.

Where Intuition Waits

In these spaces of learning and sharing, I found opportunities to connect with others on a deeper level. At wellness events, I would often set up a stall for my business as an Intuitive Somatic Mentor and Author. A divine space in the middle of all the buzz. There would be books I had written, cards I had created, and sometimes flowers laid gently across the table. But more than anything, there were conversations.

People would come by, sometimes shy, sometimes with curiosity sparkling in their eyes. They were drawn in, not always knowing why. We would start talking about something light—a book, a colour, a feeling, and then suddenly, they would pause and say, almost with a sigh, "Stacey, I just don't know what my intuition is trying to tell me."

It is one of the things I hear most often. There is this ache, this desire to know, to trust their inner wisdom. And every time I hear those words, I ask, "How is your nervous system feeling?"

There is often a moment of confusion. A tilt of the head. A blink. It seems like a strange question, especially when someone is searching for spiritual clarity or a divine nudge.

But to me, it makes perfect sense. Because intuition is not just a spiritual experience. It is a whole body experience. And your nervous system is the vessel it travels through.

Your intuition is always communicating to you. Always. It never leaves. But if your nervous system is in a state of distress, it becomes harder to hear. You might still get a sense, a flicker, but it will be buried under noise, worry, reactivity, doubt, exhaustion.

It is like trying to hear a soft melody through static. You know something beautiful is playing, but you cannot quite make out the notes. When you are a ventral vagal state, in a state of grounded presence and connection, your heart opens. Your body softens. Your mind clears. And in that space, intuition flows naturally. You remember your knowing. You do not have to force it. It rises.

However, when you are in fight or flight, frozen in a moment of disconnection or collapse, or even in a fawn state, it is not that your intuition disappears. It is just that your body is prioritising survival. And survival is loud. It makes it hard to trust anything else.

In those moments, fear tends to take the lead. And not just fear from the present, but fear braided with past wounds or future what ifs. You begin to question yourself. You ask others for answers you already have. You doubt the part of you that already knows.

However, your intuition doesn't disappear. It lives in presence, in alignment, and in your capacity to feel and receive.

And so, when someone asks me how to hear their intuition more clearly, I do not offer them a script or a strategy. I invite them back to their nervous system. I invite them to slow down, to feel, to breathe into the space that has been too tight for too long.

Because intuitive clarity does not come from trying harder. It comes from softening and safety. So next time you feel unsure or disconnected from your intuition, pause and ask yourself, "How is my nervous system in this moment?".

And instead of pushing for clarity, try meeting yourself with compassion. Ground your body, anchor your breath, and come back to the place within you that knows. Your intuition has not gone anywhere. It is just waiting for you to feel safe enough to listen.

Graceful Reminder
Intuition arrives when you are still enough to feel it, and safe enough to trust it.

A Heartfelt Pause

It was a typical afternoon, one of those days when the to-do list felt endless. I had just picked up my kids from school, and the car ride home buzzed with their overlapping voices, half-eaten snacks, and the rhythmic tapping of a restless foot against the backseat. My mind was already racing ahead, thinking about dinner, emails I hadn't responded to, and the laundry pile waiting like an uninvited guest in the corner of the house.

As I stepped through the door and opened the fridge, scanning for dinner ideas, a small voice cut through the chaos.

"Mum, are you even listening?"

I turned around and saw my daughter's face, eyes wide with that mixture of hope and hesitation, as if she wasn't sure whether her words mattered enough to pull me out of my thoughts.

In that pause, I felt it. The disconnect. My body was present, but my heart wasn't.

Instead of reacting, I took a breath. A slow, intentional inhale to the count of five, then a steady exhale. I placed my free hand gently over my heart, a subtle reminder to bring my awareness inward. I softened into the rhythm, allowing my nervous system to register safety, presence, and ease.

In what can feel like minutes, but was only mere seconds, I let my mind drift to something that always filled me with gratitude. Sunday mornings, when my kids would sneak into bed for snuggles, their small hands curling into mine. I allowed the warmth of that memory to expand, filling my heart with appreciation. Then, I looked back at my daughter and really saw her.

"I'm listening now, sweetheart," I said, meeting her gaze.

She beamed, the tension in her shoulders melting as she launched back into her story, something about a caterpillar she found at recess and how she thought it winked at her.

That moment changed everything. Not just for her, but for me.

I realised how often I moved through the day half-present, pulled between past worries and future tasks. Heart congruence isn't about waiting for the 'right' time. It's about choosing alignment in the small, ordinary moments. When I tuned into my heart, I tuned into what mattered most.

And in that brief pause, amid the hum of the dishwasher nearby, the TV being played in the next room, and the remnants of a busy day, love became the loudest thing in the room.

Practice: Heart Congruence

Find a comfortable position and invite your eyes to close if that feels safe, or lower your gaze to a gentle point in front of you. Turn your attention inwards, allowing the outer world to soften.

Begin to lengthen your breath. Inhale slowly to the count of five and exhale to the count of five. Continue this for a few breaths, then find a natural rhythm that feels supportive. With each breath, let your body know it is safe to relax.

Place two fingers or the palm of your hand over the centre of your chest, your heart space. Feel the warmth of your hand and the gentle rise and fall of your breath. This touch brings your awareness to your heart, inviting your mind to follow.

Now bring to mind something that evokes joy, gratitude, appreciation, or freedom. It might be a person, a place, a moment, or something beautifully simple from your day. There is no need to force it. Allow the feeling to naturally arise and fill your heart space.

Let yourself rest in these feelings for a few minutes. Notice how they move through your body, perhaps as warmth, lightness, or expansion. You may sense an energetic field around your heart growing stronger with each breath.

When you are ready, gently lower your hand. Take a moment to notice how you feel. Allow gentle movement in your body and softly open your eyes, carrying this sense of congruence into the rest of your day.

The Power and Wisdom of the Heart

Did you know your heart can do more than just pump blood? Inside the anatomical heart is a remarkable cluster of about 40,000 neural cells. These aren't just ordinary cells, they're organised in a way that allows the heart to function with a kind of intelligence all its own. Canadian neurologist Dr Andrew Armour discovered this sophisticated network in the early 1990s and coined the term *heart brain*. He found that the heart contains its own complex nervous system, an intricate web of neurons, neurotransmitters, proteins, and support cells, much like those found in the brain.[11] What's truly inspiring is that this heart brain has the capacity to learn, remember, feel, and sense independently of the brain in our head. This means our heart isn't just beating, it's perceiving, responding, and guiding us in ways science is only beginning to understand. It's a powerful reminder that deep inner wisdom doesn't just live in the mind. It pulses through every beat of our heart.

To truly connect with our Intuitive Intelligence®, we must first connect with our heart brain. The heart is a dynamic, intelligent centre and a powerful communication portal to the quantum field. It generates the largest electromagnetic field of any organ in the human body. One that influences not only our energy and emotions, but also the environment and people around us. In fact, the heart produces a magnetic field that is one hundred times more powerful than the one generated by the brain. This makes the heart an extraordinary source of inner wisdom, coherence, and connection.

Acting as a bridge to our non-local intuition, the heart opens a pathway to insights and knowing that extend beyond our immediate physical experience. It harmonises the grounded, embodied intuition of our physical being with the expansive, boundless intuition of the quantum field. By attuning to the intelligence of the Heart Brain, we will unlock a deeper, more profound level of guidance. One that transcends logic and reason, offering a path led by intuition, clarity, and connection.

One of the HeartMath® Institutes most compelling discoveries is the concept of heart-brain communication.[12] The heart, it turns out, sends more signals to the brain than the brain sends to the heart. These signals have a profound impact on our emotional states, cognitive functions, and even how we perceive the world around us. This raises an intriguing question, "What if we listened more to what our heart is saying, rather than letting our brain dominate?"

HeartMath®'s research also shines a light on the patterns of our heart rhythms, revealing that our emotions are closely tied to the rhythms of our heartbeat. High vibrational feeling states like joy, gratitude, and freedom create smooth, harmonious patterns, a state known as coherence. In contrast, low vibrational states like anger or frustration result in erratic, jagged rhythms. Coherence of the heart has tangible effects on our health, reducing stress and enhancing our ability to think clearly and make better decisions.[13]

Heart coherence is the physiological state where the heart, mind, and emotions are aligned and in a harmonious rhythm, often measurable through smooth heart rate variability patterns.

Heart congruence, on the other hand, is a deeper alignment where the heart's authentic desires, values, and intentions fully resonate with one's actions and life choices. Heart congruence goes beyond the physiological to encompass the emotional and spiritual realms, representing a state of true integrity and authenticity, which is why it is considered deeper.

The heart's wisdom brings hope, showing that by tuning into the heart brain and its Intuitive Intelligence® we can cultivate compassion, connection, and congruence. Through this alignment we embody grace within ourselves and the collective, one heartbeat at a time.

Graceful Reminder
The heart is not just the keeper of our pulse but the guardian of our truth. When we listen with presence, we receive more than a

beat. We receive guidance, leading us toward coherence, clarity, and connection.

Whispers of My Soul

Guided by the whispers of my soul,

I walked the path carved by intuition and courage,

I do not confirm to the worlds expectations.

Instead,

I rise in congruence with my truth,

Creating ripples of change through compassion and grace.

Presence

There is a doorway inside each of us, one that opens only in stillness. It is the doorway to presence. Before we can receive our intuition or feel the current of grace, we must first arrive in our bodies, in our breath, in this unrepeatable moment. Presence isn't passive. It is alive. It is a sacred return to the home within.

Without presence, your intuition's signal grows faint, lost amid the noise of a nervous system in survival mode. Dr Ricci-Jane Adams writes in Superconscious Intuition:[14]

*"We must be willing to cultivate presence
as part of our commitment to increasing
our access to our Intuitive Intelligence®."*

Presence invites you to pause, breathe, and return to your body and your moment. When the mind is busy reaching forward or clinging to the past, intuition gets lost. Presence clears a space. It softens the edges of urgency and allows you to really see, feel, listen, imagine, and receive.

When you practice presence, you begin to build trust in yourself. You soften. You open. You become more available to the truth already within you. You are creating enough stillness for the answers to find you. Presence doesn't mean having it all figured out. It simply means being here now with what is. The more you return to presence, the more your intuition becomes a lived experience. It no longer arrives only in moments of seeking, but becomes something you naturally are.

And when you do this, your Intuitive Intelligence® grows stronger, not overnight, but with patience and love.

Presence is the doorway through which grace flows. When we choose to be here in this breath, in this moment, we say yes to life as it is, not just as we wish it to be. In that yes, something opens. Intuition rises and grace follows. You don't need to force your way to intuition, and you don't need to earn grace. You simply return again and again to presence, to trust, to the quiet place inside where you and grace already meet.

At the end of a long day, after the whirlwind of children's laughter and tears, the flow of school routines, work responsibilities, and all the moments in between, I often find myself settling into the quiet of my bed. The world outside slows, and I lie still. I place my hand softly over the centre of my chest, right on my heart space. I close my eyes and breathe into that space, letting the weight of the day dissolve. Presence comes not as something I chase or control but as a gentle invitation. I simply rest here, allowing the stillness to hold me.

Sometimes a question rises softly, "What do I need to know right now?" Then I listen, not with my mind but with the certainty that lives beneath the noise. And in that listening, grace flows quietly, offering its wisdom. No matter how chaotic life gets, this simple ritual brings me back—to presence, to softness, to the knowing within.

Embodied Insight
What moments today invited you to step into presence, and how did grace show up when you simply allowed yourself to be still?

The Language of the Infinite

You have always held your innate intuition within you. It has never left. Not in the moments you doubted yourself. Not in the times you silenced your knowing. It waits with presence, humility, and love. Ready. As you nurture your spiritual fierceness, your willingness to be honest, vulnerable, and present, your Intuitive Intelligence® expands.

You do not need to become someone different. You only need to come home to yourself. To remember what is already yours. When you do, something shifts. You begin to speak the language of the Infinite with ease, with grace, with clarity.

There is no secret tool to uncover. No final destination. No version of you to chase. Everything you need already lives inside.

This path is not about perfection. It is about devotion. Meeting the fears that cloud your connection. Releasing them. Trusting what rises in their place. As you meet those fears with presence and loving action, they lose their hold. In the space they once filled, something ancient awakens. The language of the Infinite. A knowing that has always been yours.

Living with Intuitive Intelligence® is living with embodied grace. It moves. It transforms the way you live, love, speak, and lead. It flows through you and reaches others. It aligns you with the infinite source of creation and reminds you of what is real.

You are not separate from the Infinite.
You never were.
Now you are learning to live like it.

Graceful Reminder

You do not need to become anything else. You only need to return to the truth that has always been yours.

The Moment You Listen

There comes a moment. Sometimes it arrives as a whisper. Other times, as a roar. A pull towards change. It might begin as a quiet longing. A desire to feel more alive in your body. The curiosity to learn something new. Or simply the awareness that something in your life no longer fits. This moment is sacred. It is the voice of your intuition rising from within. A stirring that signals it is time to come home to yourself.

But walking the path of change calls for something deep. It calls for self-trust.

Self-trust is not just a decision. It is an energetic imprint. A frequency that lives in your body and radiates outward. Each time you honour your inner voice, your needs, your truth, you imprint your system with a message of safety. You remind yourself that you can be trusted. That your presence is enough. That you are safe to belong to yourself.

But let's be honest. Trust does not always arrive easily.

We are often more loyal to our fear than to our freedom. Not because we want to be, but because fear is familiar. It offers rules and structure. It promises control. It convinces us that discomfort is safer than uncertainty. That staying the same is more bearable than walking into what we cannot yet see.

And so, as you step onto this path, doubt may creep in, whispering that you are making it all up, that you are lost, that it would be safer to turn back. You may question your own sanity, feeling as though you are walking blindfolded into the unknown. At times, it may feel like a descent into darkness—what some call the *dark night of the soul*. A place where old identities dissolve, and nothing feels certain.

I know that space well.

For years, I was a police officer. It was how I introduced myself. It was how others saw me. It became how I saw myself. And while there were aspects of it that I enjoyed, it also became a container that no longer matched who I was becoming.

My intuition pulled me in a new direction. Not all at once. It came in waves.
Sometimes a whisper.
Sometimes a restless night.
Sometimes a flash of clarity that passed quickly but left a deep imprint.

At first, I resisted. I questioned it. I told myself I should be content. I had built something solid. Something people respected.

But deep down, I could feel it. The life I had built was no longer in alignment with the truth of who I was.

Letting go of that identity felt like standing on the edge of a cliff. It felt like walking away from structure, purpose, and familiarity. But what I came to understand was that letting go was not about losing something. It was about making space.

Space to rediscover myself.
Space to breathe.
Space to meet the parts of me I had long forgotten.
And in that space, I met something profound.

Grace.

Grace held me in the unravelling.

It reminded me that I did not need to have it all figured out. That I could be safe in the uncertainty. That I could trust the path, even when I could not see the full picture. Grace was not something I had to earn. It was always there. In the quiet. In the breath. In the moments I allowed myself to soften instead of strive.

This is Embodied Grace.

It is not just a feeling. It is a lived experience. A felt sense in the body that says, "You are held." It invites you to stop gripping, to stop proving, and to come back to your centre.

When grace and self-trust meet within us, something powerful happens.
We begin to expand.
Not through force, but through presence.
Not through perfection, but through truth.
Not because we have all the answers, but because we are willing to listen.

Self-trust creates the energetic foundation. Grace allows us to soften into it.
Together, they open us to deeper healing and fuller expansion.

So if you are standing at the edge of change, know,
You are not lost.
You are being invited into alignment.
Your intuition is already guiding you.
Your body already knows.
Self-trust is the imprint you are creating.
Grace is the presence that holds you as you do.

The only question is this.
Will you listen?

Embodied Insight

*If you weren't afraid of losing a part of yourself, what new
possibilities might open up for you?*

Flowing with Trust

Intuition is not a tool we use only when life feels heavy or when we're standing at a crossroads, desperately searching for answers. It's not something that we tap into sporadically, like a crutch to lean on during the tough times. No, intuition is an ever-present guide, constantly inviting us into the rhythm of grace. It is a steady companion, not just when we seek clarity on life's big questions, but in the small, everyday moments too.

Our intuition speaks to us in many ways, sometimes softly, other times with urgency, but always in ways that require our attention. It's that subtle nudge to take the long way home, even though the shorter route is just fine. It's the instinctive pull to pause and listen to the sound of the birds outside your window, or to stop and breathe deeply as you walk through a park. It's the quiet knowing that something small but meaningful can shift in our lives if we simply follow a subtle hunch, like choosing the less travelled path or speaking our truth, even when it feels uncomfortable.

Listening to our intuition is like cultivating a relationship. It's not a one-off experience that we can dip in and out of when it's convenient. It's a constant invitation to grace, offered to us each day, in every little decision we make. From the moment we wake up to the second we close our eyes at night, we are presented with opportunities to tune in and align with that inner knowing.

Take, for example, the simple act of choosing a route home. Maybe your usual route is straightforward, familiar, and quick. But one day, something within you nudges you to take a different street, one you've never considered before. It seems like a small thing, but what if that detour is the space where magic happens? Maybe the new route gives you a moment of quiet you didn't expect, or you stumble upon a hidden café that sparks a moment of joy. The simple act of following your intuition leads to a small gift. A gift of presence, of discovery, of slowing down enough to notice.

The same goes for moments throughout the day where you feel the pull to listen, to what your body needs, to what your heart desires, to what your soul craves. The invitation of grace in these moments is about trusting yourself, even in the small, unspoken choices. Choosing to honour your intuition, no matter how mundane the task, brings you closer to a life filled with alignment. When you trust yourself in the tiny moments, you begin to trust yourself in the bigger ones. You build a foundation of faith that is unshakable, rooted in the knowledge that you can rely on your inner guidance every step of the way.

Listening to your intuition may feel unfamiliar at first, like learning a new language. It can feel awkward or uncertain, not because it is unclear but because it moves differently than the noise you are used to. Intuition isn't about getting it right, it's about presence. It's about listening, even when you aren't sure what you're listening for. The more you practise, the clearer the voice becomes. The higher the frequency you can access, the easier it is to translate the message, and the more effortless it feels to follow. It's as if you begin to hear that inner wisdom more clearly, more boldly, and trust it more deeply. And the more you act on it, the more the universe responds in kind.

Intuition is not some mysterious force outside of ourselves. It's our own voice, our own wisdom, woven into the fabric of our being. And just like any relationship, we need to nurture it. We must pay attention, lean in, and embrace it daily. It's not always about having all the answers. Sometimes, intuition is just about the invitation, the inner voice that says, "Trust this moment. Trust yourself."

There are days when the world feels loud, chaotic, or uncertain, and it's easy to drown out the quiet voice inside. But every time we make the choice to pause and listen, we are affirming to ourselves that we trust our own inner compass. We honour the wisdom that lies within, not only in moments of crisis but in every quiet, ordinary second of our lives.

This is where true grace resides. It's in the willingness to listen, to take the path less travelled, to choose the detour, to follow the hunch. The grace of intuition isn't just in life's major decisions, it's in the everyday invitations to trust, to show up, and to allow ourselves to be guided with ease. It's in those little moments where we choose alignment over fear, presence over distraction, and peace over rushing.

So, what would it look like if you listened to your intuition more consistently, even in the smallest decisions? What would it feel like to surrender to the flow of grace that's being offered to you every day, in each whisper, nudge, and pull?

Trust the journey. Trust the process. Trust that your intuition is always there, guiding you, not just when life feels overwhelming but in every beautiful, simple moment in between. And with each choice you make from that place of grace, you will begin to witness how your life unfolds in beautiful, unexpected ways. Ways that are guided by the wisdom that has always been inside of you.

Graceful Reminder

We don't wait for intuition to arrive. It is already here, breathing with us through the ordinary, inviting grace into every corner of our day.

PART FIVE

Expand Capacity for Love

Love is our Natural State

Love is our natural state, a current that flows through us, connecting us to ourselves, others, and the world. Yet, life's challenges and conditioning often disrupt this flow, creating barriers that limit our ability to give and receive love freely. These barriers can arise from societal expectations about what love should look like, family dynamics that left us questioning our worth, or painful experiences that taught us to guard our hearts.

I remember standing at my dad's funeral when I was twelve, trying to make sense of something too big for my body to hold. People spoke of love and loss, but all I felt was confusion and a strange emptiness I did not know how to name. Over the years, I began to associate love with disappearance, as something that could be taken away without warning. A belief took root that day: love was fragile, conditional, and had to be earned to stay.

This belief shaped my life quietly but profoundly. I pushed myself to achieve and overextended in relationships, silencing my needs, believing that love was something I had to prove myself worthy of. No matter how much I gave or achieved, the feeling of being truly loved never came. There was always an ache inside me, a fear that if I stopped striving, love would disappear.

Then came a moment of reckoning. I was nineteen, not long after Grant and I had started dating. Exhausted not just physically but emotionally and mentally, I felt disconnected from myself. One night, sitting on the edge of my bed, I realised I could no longer hide my pain. Grant entered the room and asked if I was okay. Every part of me wanted to say yes, to stay small and silent. But something inside me cracked open. I let the tears rise and spill over. I said, "I am not okay and I do not know what I need."

It felt terrifying. I worried I was too much, too messy. But I stayed with it, with myself. And to my surprise, he stayed too. No fixing, no judgement, just presence. A hand on my back, a quiet moment of being held without needing to perform or prove. That night, I felt what it was like to be loved in my vulnerability, not despite it, but because I allowed it to be seen.

At first, this realisation felt foreign. Years of conditioning do not unravel overnight. Yet, I approached my old belief with curiosity rather than resistance. What if I did not have to prove my worth? What if I was already enough?

A deep shift followed. The tightness I had carried in my chest softened, the weight I had been unknowingly bearing lightened. My body, once accustomed to guarding against vulnerability, began to recognise safety. My shoulders loosened, my breath deepened, and subtle tremors of release reminded me that my nervous system could hold love as easily as it had held tension. Love was not something I had to chase or fight for, it was something I could allow myself to receive, to rest in, right here, right now.

Our nervous system is not just a vessel for stress and trauma, it is where we can learn to hold love for ourselves, for others, and for the world. When we create safety within, we open the door to intuition, the guidance that invites us to soften, to be kind, and to open our hearts. This guidance resonates deeply in the body, speaking the language of connection, compassion, and unconditional love. As we cultivate inner safety, we allow ourselves to experience the full spectrum of emotions and the profound love we deserve.

The limitations we encounter along the way are not faults, they are adaptive responses developed in the face of pain. Meeting these barriers with compassion rather than judgement softens the walls that once kept us from feeling more and loving more. This journey is both emotional and physiological. When we intentionally create safety within, we signal to our body that it is okay to open, to trust, and to receive love, not as a reward for achievement, but as our natural state.

As we attune to our nervous system, cultivate inner safety, and surrender to our intuitive intelligence, we allow ourselves to hold both the tender love we have for ourselves and the richness of connection with others. A love that knows no limits. This is the foundation of healing, connection, and living with an open heart.

Expanding our capacity for love is not about stretching the edges of an existing space. It is about creating new space from within. Love is not something we try to fit into the confines of who we already are. It is a gentle unfolding that arises when we soften the inner walls built from fear, protection, and past pain. As we meet ourselves with compassion, new chambers of the heart open, places we may not have known existed. This expansion does not come through effort or striving, but through grace. The more we allow ourselves to be present with what is, the more love finds room to flow naturally, filling the spaces once occupied by contraction and defence.

Graceful Reminder

*The heart expands when met with kindness. Begin with yourself
and love will ripple outward, softening old barriers, deepening
connection, and reminding you that love was never outside of you,
but within you all along.*

Softening into Love

From an early age, many of us internalise a belief that love is conditional:
"I am loved when I achieve."
"I am lovable only if I please others."
"I must fit in to be worthy of connection."

These messages shape how we show up in relationships. We may strive for perfection, suppress our true feelings, or fear being vulnerable. While these behaviours may have protected us in the past, they can leave us feeling disconnected and unseen in the present.

Simone, a client of mine, spent years believing that love had to be earned. She excelled in her career, constantly proving her worth through achievement, yet deep down, she felt an emptiness that no accolade could fill. In our sessions, she began to notice how this conditioning had shaped not only her relationships but her relationship with herself, a subtle but constant whisper of "not enough" that lingered in her body.

Through our work together, Simone began to reconnect with herself, especially the part of her that had felt unseen or unworthy as a child. She allowed herself to sit with the tension in her chest and shoulders and imagine holding that younger Simone tenderly. She offered reassurance to the scared, striving child inside her: I see you. I am here. You do not have to earn love to exist. Slowly, she began to notice the subtle tremors and heaviness in her body, meeting them with warmth rather than judgment.

As Simone tended to this inner self, she began to understand that the compulsion to earn love was not a personal failing, but a conditioned response. She practised speaking kindly to the younger part of her, acknowledging the fear and longing that had driven her for so long. In doing so, her body began to soften, sensing that it could finally relax into safety and hold love, rather than brace against its absence.

With this internal presence, Simone's life began to shift. She no longer clung to approval or validation, yet she felt more connected than ever. She could respond with compassion rather than anxiety, feel the guidance of her intuition, and recognise that she was inherently worthy of love and belonging.

The shift was not sudden, but a lived, ongoing experience. Each time Simone noticed the warmth in her body and the subtle ease that arose, she was reminded of the truth she had always carried. Love is not a prize to be won or a reward for doing enough. It flows naturally when we feel safe in our bodies and trust our inner guidance, showing up in the way we care for ourselves, the choices we make, and the connections we nurture. In this space, love is not earned or measured. It simply radiates from within, shaping every part of our lives.

Embodied Insight

Where in my life do, I still feel I need to prove my worth to receive love?
Who would I be if I no longer believed love had to be earned?

Love Through Vulnerability

Love asks us to take risks, not the reckless kind, but the deeply human act of being truly seen. Vulnerability is the doorway through which love flows, yet it can feel terrifying because it exposes us. What if I'm rejected? What if I'm misunderstood?

The more we try to shield ourselves from pain, the more we close ourselves off from love. True strength lies in vulnerability, the courage to say, "Here I am, with all my fears and imperfections, and I am still worthy of connection."

When I opened my service as an Intuitive Somatic Mentor, it was one of the most vulnerable steps I've ever taken. Moving away from frontline policing and stepping into a role so different from what I had known felt like walking into the unknown. I worried about how my family, friends, and even former police colleagues would perceive me. I was concerned about people from my past, those friends I hadn't spoken to since school, who now saw me on Facebook - what would they think of me? Would they misunderstand what I was doing?

There was so much fear, but also so much love. I had to choose love, to step into vulnerability with the courage to be seen. It was big. It was uncomfortable. It was messy. And it was worth it. Because by embracing my vulnerability, I found people. People who found me, and together, we remember we are not alone.

Vulnerability is a practice, not a onetime event. By choosing openness and love over fear, we increase our capacity to love and be loved. But this process isn't just emotional, it's deeply somatic. Our bodies hold the imprints of past wounds, times we felt unseen or unheard, and the ways we've learnt to protect ourselves from further pain.

To embrace vulnerability is to invite our nervous system into safety, to gently remind ourselves that it is okay to be seen, to be heard, and to be fully present in love.

When we allow ourselves to be vulnerable, we create space for authentic connection. And it is in that sacred space that love thrives, not as a transaction, but as a shared experience of grace. Vulnerability doesn't just open the door to others, it opens the door to our own hearts, and it is here that the deepest love is born.

As you expand your capacity for love, you transform the way you relate to yourself and others. You notice that love is not a scarce resource, but is infinite that grows with use. Giving yourself permission to love and be loved radiates a sense of grace that inspires others to do the same.

This journey is not about perfection, it is about practice. Each time you choose kindness over criticism, connection over fear, and openness over defence, you are rewriting the narrative of what love can be. And as your nervous system anchors in safety, the current of love flows more freely, guiding you toward deeper connection and a life rooted in grace.

Practice: The Courage to Be Seen

Find a quiet place where you can sit comfortably and feel supported. Allow your body to settle and take a moment to arrive. Place one hand on your heart and the other on your belly. Breathe in slowly through your nose, feeling the space beneath your hands rise. Exhale softly through your mouth, allowing your body to relax with each breath.

When you feel ready, gently bring to mind a moment when you allowed yourself to be vulnerable. It might be a time you spoke your truth, shared your feelings, or took a brave step forward. There is no need to search too deeply. Whatever comes is enough.

Notice what you feel in your body as you remember this moment. Perhaps your breath shifts, or you sense warmth, tightness, or movement. Simply notice, without needing to change anything.

Gently use the fingertips from one hand to tap on the centre of your chest, in your heart space. Say to yourself, out loud or within your mind, "It is safe to be seen." Repeat this as many times as needed, allowing your body to receive and embody the words.

When you are ready, take a final slow breath. Feel your feet or the surface beneath you. Notice how your body feels now. Acknowledge the courage it takes to be seen, and remind yourself that vulnerability is not weakness. It is an opening toward deeper connection.

Holding Yourself With Kindness

Before my journey with Embodied Grace, my internal critic was loud and unrelenting. I remember nights when my mind raced with harsh judgements, telling me I wasn't enough, that I had to fix everything before I could deserve kindness or rest. Offering myself gentleness felt like a distant, impossible idea.

One evening, after a particularly heavy day with the kids unsettled, their voices louder than usual, and my patience wearing thin, I finally sat down feeling utterly drained. I sat quietly with the tightness in my chest and the heaviness weighing on my shoulders. Instead of pushing these feelings away like I always did, I paused and asked myself, "Can I allow myself to be human right now, with all my fears and imperfections?" It was a small, shaky question, but it opened a door.

I first noticed the physical sensations, the knot in my gut and the tension across my back as messages from my body asking for care, not punishment. I realised that being kind to myself did not mean denying the pain or rushing to fix it. It was about staying present with discomfort without turning away.

So, I kept asking, "Am I deserving of kindness even when I feel broken?" Slowly, the answer began to shift from a whisper to a steady voice of, Yes. I was worthy of love and care, simply because I existed.

This was not an easy or quick transformation. When the inner critic was dominant in my life, I asked myself these questions every day. It was a daily practice of choosing to meet myself with gentleness in moments when I wanted to turn away or hide. I asked myself, "How am I speaking to myself right now?" and "What do I need to feel cared for in this moment?" Each time I answered, I created a little more space for healing and self-acceptance.

Choosing kindness, especially during the struggle, felt radical. It challenged everything I thought I knew about worthiness and strength. But through this practice, I discovered that true healing begins not when we fix ourselves, but when we hold ourselves with compassion, no matter how messy or painful the moment.

If you are wondering how to begin, try asking yourself these questions. Can I allow myself to be human right now? Can I meet my pain with the same compassion I would offer a friend? Am I deserving of kindness even in my darkest moments?

Choosing kindness, especially in times of struggle, is a radical choice. It is a powerful act of courage that breaks the cycle of self-criticism and perfectionism. This choice opens the way to healing and helps you build a new relationship with yourself. One grounded in gentleness and acceptance, no matter what you are facing.

These questions and this choice can be your guide as you learn to hold yourself with kindness exactly as you are.

Graceful Reminder
*Accepting the invitation to be with yourself is accepting the call to
expand in love and presence.*

Chasing Relief, Losing Me

Through my teenage years and well into my thirties, I discovered that I could avoid and numb my emotions by drinking alcohol. It started as a casual habit: too stressed—drink a glass of wine. Bad day at work—have a glass of bourbon. But as my responsibilities increased, especially during my years as a frontline detective in the Police Force, it became more than that. Stress was a constant companion, and every day seemed to offer a reason to drink. Mornings were a flurry of getting my four kids ready, dropping them at school, and heading into a high-pressure job where I faced intense situations daily. Drinking became a scheduled mission of its own, something I looked forward to at the end of every difficult day.

I convinced myself I didn't have a problem. But avoiding my emotions and numbing them because they felt too overwhelming to face took a toll on my wellbeing and fed into a shame spiral, I didn't yet understand. There were times I would stop drinking for a few weeks, yet whenever I started again, it would be with a vengeance, as if I were trying to drown emotions that seemed too big to meet on my own.

For years, I toyed with the idea of quitting, what is now referred to as 'sober curiosity.' Yet every time I hit a rough patch or felt flooded by anger, sadness, or guilt, I reached back for the familiar escape. The true challenge arose during the sober moments that followed those drinking episodes. When I was sober, the weight of self-judgement would crush me. I was often the unkindest to myself then, berating myself for what I saw as failures and shortcomings. I felt undeserving of love and kindness, spiralling deeper into self-criticism and shame.

It was only when I began learning to meet myself with kindness that I started breaking this cycle. I realised that what I truly needed was not to drown out my pain but to sit with it, to hold it with compassion, and to recognise my struggles as deserving of gentleness, not punishment. This shift opened a door to a different way of relating to myself, a way that acknowledged my humanity and the complexity of my emotions. I learnt that holding myself with kindness was not a sign of weakness but a powerful act of courage, allowing me to embrace my imperfections and navigate my journey with grace.

Learning to nurture myself with kindness, to show up for my pain instead of escaping it, was a journey, and not always an easy one. But with time, it has become a practice of radical acceptance that holds me in a way that alcohol never could.

Practice: Breath of Kindness

Find a comfortable place to sit or lie down. Soften your gaze or close your eyes. Take a slow breath in through your nose, inviting kindness into your body, and exhale through your mouth with a sigh of release. Let each breath create more space for ease.

Continue breathing naturally. With each inhale, welcome kindness; with each exhale, release what you no longer need.

Bring your attention to your heart. Take a gentle breath and quietly say, I still like you. Notice one small reason you like yourself—your courage, kindness, the way you show up, or something else.

Take another breath and say, I still love you. Let a reason arise naturally. Then breathe and say, I love you because... Allow whatever comes to mind to be enough.

Stay here a few moments, noticing how your body feels. There is no right or wrong. When you are ready, take a final breath, feel the support beneath you, and acknowledge the kindness you've offered yourself. Carry this compassion with you, knowing you can return to this breath anytime.

Kind Versus Nice

From a young age, many of us, particularly women, are taught the importance of being 'nice.' 'Be nice to your siblings.' 'Be nice to the boys.' 'Be nice to your boss.' 'Be nice to everyone.' This societal conditioning often leaves little room for nuance or authenticity. Over time, being nice becomes synonymous with suppressing our own needs, silencing our voices, and prioritising the comfort of others over our own truth. Even when kindness is mentioned, it often feels like a misnomer. What people really seem to mean is, 'Be nice, don't make waves, don't challenge, don't disrupt.'

There is a profound difference between being kind and being nice, especially in how we treat ourselves. Understanding this distinction can transform the way we navigate self-care and self-compassion.

Being nice to yourself often involves seeking immediate comfort and avoiding discomfort at all costs. It is the voice that says, "You have had a hard day, just binge-watch another episode and forget about everything." Or the one that encourages you to push down difficult emotions, to plaster on a smile and tell yourself, "It is fine, everything is fine." Being nice might feel soothing in the moment, but it tends to prioritise short-term ease over long-term wellbeing.

While there is nothing wrong with occasional indulgences or choosing the path of least resistance, being nice tends to keep us on the surface. It can prevent us from addressing deeper needs, making hard choices, or growing in meaningful ways. At its core, being nice is about temporary relief, not lasting care.

Kindness, on the other hand, is an act of true compassion. It involves meeting yourself where you are with honesty and understanding while also creating and holding space for your highest self. Kindness does not shy away from discomfort or difficult truths. Instead, it asks, "What do I truly need right now?" and "How can I best support myself, even if it is not the easiest path?"

Being kind might mean setting a boundary when your energy is depleted, even if it feels uncomfortable in the moment. It might look like allowing yourself to feel and process difficult emotions, rather than pushing them aside. Kindness could mean choosing to take a walk in nature instead of numbing out on your phone because you know fresh air will nurture your spirit.

Kindness sees the bigger picture. It is not about quick fixes or surface-level peace. It is about cultivating a deeper connection with yourself and creating a foundation of care that truly sustains you. It is about saying, "I deserve more than a temporary escape. I deserve real, lasting support."

When I worked as a detective, balancing family life with my career was no easy feat. My husband worked long hours, and we were raising four kids, each with their own unique needs. I often carried the fear that I was not doing enough as a mother, that somehow I was falling short. There were moments when the weight of responsibility felt almost unbearable, and I questioned whether I could truly meet the needs of my children while still caring for myself.

I worked part-time, doing three shifts a week instead of four, but my workload was just as demanding as any full-time officer's. I found myself taking on more and more responsibilities, partly because I felt like I had something to prove. A subconscious fear clung to me, the fear that I was not good enough. I fuelled this fear until it was suffocating. I believed that if I did not push myself harder, I would not measure up. Even though I was working part-time, I felt the need to show everyone—my colleagues, my family, and myself—that I could be both a great detective and a dedicated mother.

As the work piled up, so did the pressure. But even as I felt more and more overwhelmed, I kept telling myself and others that everything was fine when in reality it was not. I had fallen into my old patterns of people-pleasing and perfectionism, trying to do it all and never wanting to let anyone down. I was avoiding the tough emotions building inside me by numbing out with alcohol and binge eating. I did not want to deal with the hard choices I knew I needed to make, especially around my future as a police officer. I kept avoiding the conflict because I knew deep down I needed to establish boundaries, but I was terrified of what that might mean.

Through the work I was doing to support my nervous system, I came to a realisation. I could not keep running from these fears. I had to face the underlying belief that I was not good enough or that I would fail. These fears had been shaping everything I did and how I showed up in the world. I knew that if I kept trying to be nice to myself and others, I would only stay stuck and eventually burn out. I made a decision. I needed to be kind to myself.

That meant stopping the cycle of numbing and pushing away my feelings. I allowed myself to pause, to sit with the discomfort, and to give myself permission to feel. By supporting my nervous system and making space for playfulness and devotion, I started to find the balance I had been craving. I set clear boundaries, prioritising my family and my wellbeing. I transferred to a different unit, still as a detective, but one that offered the family life balance I longed for. For the first time in a long time, I felt a sense of freedom. The relief I felt in that shift was like a weight lifting from my shoulders.

Every time I felt the temptation to just be nice, to ignore my needs for the sake of others, I would hug myself and ask, "What would kindness look like in this moment?"

Making the shift from being nice to being kind requires courage and intention. It means letting go of societal pressures to please others, to avoid discomfort, and to always put others first. It requires us to honour our own needs even when it feels difficult or uncomfortable. It is about practising self-respect, self-trust, and ultimately, self-love.

Being nice might soothe the surface, but being kind nourishes your soul. You, in all your beautiful complexity, deserve nothing less than that depth of care.

Graceful Reminder

To be kind to yourself is to claim your own presence, to honour your body, and to meet your soul with the care and grace it has always deserved.

Embracing The Learning Curve

In the early days, shopping with my twins was manageable. They would sit in the pram or double trolley while I went about my errands. But as they grew older, too big for the pram or trolley, they needed to walk beside me, and things became more challenging. My son, especially, would get easily distracted by anything shiny or exciting in the store. He would wander off, and his love for hide-and-seek would sometimes catch me off guard.

One day, I turned away for just a moment, and when I looked back, he was gone. Panic gripped me as I called his name, searching through the aisles. After what felt like an eternity, I found him hiding behind a clothes rack, giggling and yelling, "You found me! Your turn!" I was in the middle of a game of hide-and-seek that I hadn't even known we were playing.

Initially, I was hard on myself. I berated myself for not being more vigilant, for not keeping a better eye on him. I tried to be 'nice' to get through the rest of the shopping trip, pushing the discomfort and overwhelm aside, pretending everything was fine. But when we finally got in my car I broke down in tears. When I got home, I took a moment to pause. I hugged my son tightly, allowing that hug to serve as co-regulation for both of us. As I held him, I took a deep breath, reminding myself that this was part of his world. I was learning just as he was.

Instead of continuing to beat myself up, I decided to be kind to myself. I acknowledged that this situation was new for both of us, and I was doing the best I could at the time. I reminded myself that this wasn't about perfection, it was about understanding and compassion. For him, yes, but also for myself. I recognised the overwhelm I felt and honoured the love and care I gave to my children, even in the midst of the chaos.

That night I wrote myself a letter full of kindness a compassionate inner voice reminding me that it is okay not to have everything figured out. I acknowledged that I am doing my best and that I deserve kindness within offering myself the care and understanding I needed. Writing that letter felt incredibly nourishing like a quiet balm soothing my overwhelmed heart. It also expanded my capacity for love not just for my children but for myself. By allowing myself this kindness I opened a deeper space to hold all parts of my experience with gentleness and grace.

Extending kindness to ourselves can be deeply healing. Writing a letter from a place of understanding and compassion allows you to acknowledge your experiences and emotions without judgement. This practice nurtures self-compassion and invites you to embrace your journey with love and acceptance.

Embodied Insight

Take a moment to connect with your heart. What words of kindness and understanding does your inner voice want to share with you today? Imagine writing a letter to yourself from a place of compassion, acknowledging your efforts and offering the care you need. Notice how this simple act of self-kindness feels in your body.

Our Greatest Teachers

In my journey of living with an open heart, I have found that some of my greatest teachers of grace have been children, both my own and those I've met along the way. You do not need to have birthed a child for a child to be your teacher. Children, in their rawness and purity, reflect back to us the truths we forget, the patience we lose and the love that's always there. Each of my four children has, in their own way, been a teacher of grace in my life. Not because they try to be, but simply because they are. They invite me into presence, humility and loving action, stretching my capacity for love and reminding me what it means to be human. Through them, I have learnt to soften, surrender and see grace in the messiness of life.

Children live in the now. They do not dwell in yesterday or worry about tomorrow the way we do. My children have taught me the sacredness of the present moment. Whether it is the way they marvel at a bug on the ground or how they ask endless questions before bed, they show me that life is happening right now. They pull me from thought into body, into the space where grace waits.

Adeline, with her deep, curious eyes and endless wonder, reminds me daily that presence is the greatest gift we can offer. Not just to others but to ourselves. The moment I slip into busyness or distraction, she will feel it. And without judgement, she will pull me back with a simple, "Mummy, are you listening?" It is grace in its purest form, an invitation to return to the now.

Parenting, caregiving or simply being in the presence of children can stir every unhealed part of us. They have an uncanny ability to press on the tender spots, the places where we still hold tightness, fear or old wounds. Rhiannon, with her fierce independence and unshakable sense of self, has been my greatest mirror. Her refusal to bend to people-pleasing patterns me to examine where I still do.

Her ability to express emotions freely makes me question where I still suppress my own.

Grace shows up in these moments too, not in perfect responses, but in the willingness to see the lesson. Reminding me that healing is not about always getting it right, it's about making space for growth, repair, and letting love be stronger than fear. Before having children, I thought love had limits—certain thresholds of capacity, patience or endurance. My children have shattered every notion about how big love can be. Each one, in their unique way, has expanded my heart beyond measure.

Ashton, with his gentle spirit and deep empathy, has taught me about the kind of love that sees beyond behaviour. The kind that holds space for big emotions and mistakes. The kind that stays when things feel heavy. He reminds me that grace is found not just in joyful moments but in challenging ones too. Through his love for animals of all kinds, I've learnt that this same unconditional love applies to all beings—he teaches me to love fully, without judgement, and to hold space for others' experiences, no matter how difficult they may seem.

Vanessa, with her nurturing heart and patience, teaches me about the quiet strength of love. She moves through the world with a kindness that is both gentle and powerful. Whether it is the way she instinctively comforts her siblings or how she offers her time so freely to those in need, she reminds me that love is an action. That grace is found in the smallest gestures of care, in the moments when we choose to be there for each other, not from duty, but desire.

Love, when embodied fully, is boundless. It makes room for all that we are. And children, in their unconditional way of loving, show us this truth again and again. Perhaps one of the greatest lessons my children have gifted me is the understanding that grace is found in imperfection. The mess, the chaos, the moments where patience runs thin, these are the spaces where grace meets us.

I have had days where I have fallen short, where my voice has been sharper than intended, where exhaustion has dulled my ability to be fully present. And yet, my children never withhold their love. They don't demand perfection from me. Instead, they show me the beauty of repair, of trying again, of saying I'm sorry and I love you in the same breath. Through them, I have learnt that grace is not about getting it right all the time, it is about being willing to show up, to love through the mess, to keep choosing connection over perfection.

Every child, whether ours or another's, holds wisdom we can learn from. They teach us what it means to live with an open heart, to embrace wonder, to let love be the guiding force. They remind us that grace is not something we must strive for, it is something we allow ourselves to receive and give.

I am endlessly grateful for my children, for the ways they continue to shape me, stretch me and call me deeper into grace. They are my greatest teachers, not because I teach them, but because they show me, again and again, how to be.

Embodied Insight
Reflect on a time when you were in the presence of a child. What did they teach you in that moment about presence, humility, or loving action? How can you apply that lesson to your own life today?

Learning to Love

Growing up, I didn't know how to love my body. For much of my life, I viewed my body as something to control, fight against, or, at best, ignore. I danced throughout my childhood, and within that world, I often felt like my body was being compared to others. That's when I began to compare myself, too. I would look at other people and see what seemed like effortless beauty, self-assuredness, and grace. I wondered why I couldn't embody that same sense of ease in my skin. Instead, my body felt foreign, something separate from me, almost like a burden I had to carry through life. It wasn't that I hated my body. I wasn't quite sure how to feel about it at all. I simply didn't know how to connect with it in a loving way.

There were moments when I tried to take care of it, but my efforts were driven by a desire to change it into something it wasn't, to force it into moulds that weren't true to its natural state. I spent years pushing my body in ways that were disconnected from its real needs. I didn't listen when it told me to rest. Instead, I pushed through fatigue. I didn't honour its cues for nourishment. Instead, I would try to follow rigid rules of what I should eat, when, and how much. But more often than not, I'd end up overindulging, swaying to the other side and eating everything in sight. I had been taught to believe that my value was tied to my appearance, my size, my ability to meet an external standard of beauty. And so, loving my body felt like an impossible task, because I wasn't loving it—I was loving what I hoped it would become.

The idea of truly loving my body didn't make sense to me because I had been taught to reject it. I was taught to focus on what was wrong with it, to see it as a project, something that could be fixed or improved. If there were things I didn't like about myself—my weight, my shape, my skin—I tried to change them, believing that once I did, I would finally feel worthy, finally feel loved. But that approach only deepened the sense of disconnection between me and my body.

As I grew older, the strain of this relationship only intensified. I'd swing from periods of intense self-discipline, obsessive dieting, over-exercising, and controlling what I ate, to moments of indulgence, where I numbed out the discomfort with things like alcohol or unhealthy foods. I didn't understand it at the time, but in each phase, I was running from something deeper. I was running from the pain of not feeling good enough, of not knowing how to love myself fully, especially my body.

When I removed both alcohol and excessive exercise at the same time, my nervous system was left without the usual coping mechanisms it had grown accustomed to. My body, in a state of stress, relied on these habits for survival, whether it's the stimulation of alcohol or the constant motion of over-exercising. When both were taken away, my nervous system had to adjust, but it didn't immediately know how to find balance. As a result, my system shifted into a dorsal vagal state (freeze or disconnection). This meant I found myself not engaging in any activity at all, reflecting a deep sense of fatigue and a lack of drive. My body didn't know how to move from a heightened state of survival to one of calm, and it resulted in a feeling of disconnection and low energy.

I had to return to the foundations and rebuild safety within my nervous system before I could fully face the uncomfortable emotions and fears once again. While I am truly proud of myself for stopping the over-exercising and drinking alcohol, in hindsight, I wish I had sought support to integrate more strategies for nervous system regulation, rather than trying to navigate it all on my own. This process of rebuilding safety also led me to realise something profound. For most of my life, I had been looking at my body with eyes of criticism, not love. I had been trying to mould it into something I thought it should be, instead of accepting it for it as it was. And in that acceptance, I found a new kind of freedom.

As I embarked on the journey of expanding my capacity for love, I started to recognise that the way I had treated my body mirrored the way I had treated my heart. I had been withholding love from myself, thinking that I had to earn it or that it was conditional on how I appeared or how I behaved. I didn't realise that love—true love—is not something to be earned. It's something to be experienced in the present moment, no matter where I stood or what my body looked like.

This realisation was both powerful and humbling. I began to see that I had to stop seeing my body as a project or a problem. It was not a puzzle to be fixed, it was a part of me that deserved the same love and care that I offered to others. I had to stop treating it as an enemy, as something separate from me, and start viewing it as a partner, a companion that had been with me through every step of my life, doing its best to carry me, protect me, and support me.

The process of expanding my capacity for love meant that I had to extend compassion to the parts of my body I had ignored or rejected for so long. It meant looking at the weight I had gained without judgement, seeing it not as a failure but as a result of years of pushing my body to its limits. It meant choosing to nourish myself not just with food, but with kindness, patience, and acceptance. I had to let go of the belief that I had to 'fix' myself in order to be worthy of love.

Each day, I practised loving my body in small ways. I stopped seeing it as an obstacle to be overcome and started seeing it as a reflection of my growth, my healing, and my journey. I began to listen to its cues, honouring its needs for rest, nourishment, and movement. I started speaking to myself with gentleness, instead of harsh criticism. I began to see my body as a living, breathing expression of my soul, worthy of love exactly as it is.

This process was not always easy, and there were days when I slipped back into old patterns of judgement. But each time, I chose to begin again. I learnt that expanding my capacity for love wasn't about perfection, it was about practice. It was about choosing to love my body, even when I didn't fully understand it, even when it didn't fit my expectations.

As I continue on this journey, I am learning that love is not something I have to chase or work toward, it is already within me, waiting to be extended to all parts of myself. My body is not something to be fixed. It is a sacred part of who I am, deserving of care, respect, and love. And as I expand my capacity for love, I know that I am also expanding my capacity to love others, to show up in the world with a heart that is open, compassionate, and free from the limitations I once placed on myself.

So, as you walk your own journey of expanding your capacity for love, I invite you to look at your body through new eyes. Not as something to be controlled, fixed, or changed, but as a beautiful, sacred part of you. The journey to true self-love is not about perfection, it's about acceptance, compassion, and the willingness to embrace yourself as you are, right now. And in that embrace, you will find the love that has always been there, waiting for you to recognise it.

Embodied Insight
What would it look like to let go of the belief that you have to do everything on your own? How can you begin to share your journey with others, knowing that it's okay to seek help and guidance along the way?

PART SIX

Beneath the Surface

Opening the Door

When was the last time you truly allowed yourself to feel an emotion—fully, without judgment or resistance? For many of us, emotions are something we manage, suppress, or avoid. We live in a world that tells us to "keep it together," but there is wisdom in simply feeling, in meeting what arises with curiosity and care.

I remember working with a client who, for years, had learned to push away anything that didn't feel "acceptable." She bottled up anger, shame, and sadness, feeling guilty for even experiencing them. In our sessions together, we first focused on helping her feel a sense of safety and resource within her body—breathing, grounding, and noticing supportive sensations. Only once she felt anchored could we slow down and notice the sensations as emotions arose. I guided her to sit with the feeling, simply witnessing it without judgment or the need to fix it. That small act—giving herself permission—was transformative. It wasn't about solving or changing anything, just noticing and being fully present with what was there.

Opening the door to our emotions doesn't happen by force. It begins with offering ourselves permission, gently, to feel and allowing what arises to move through us. This practice is a cornerstone of embodying grace. When we witness our emotions with compassion, we create space for healing, insight, and deeper self-connection.

For many of us, feeling can feel unfamiliar, uncomfortable, or even unsafe. We may have learned to suppress emotions to protect ourselves from pain or vulnerability. And yet, when we deny them, we also deny the chance to heal, to grow, and to reconnect with ourselves. In sessions, we often explore where emotions are held—tightness in the chest, heaviness in the gut, tension in the jaw—and bring gentle awareness to these sensations.

Emotions carry energy, and each has a natural quality in the body. Some emotions, like fear, shame, anger, or sadness, feel dense, heavy, or contracting. These low-vibration states are not wrong or bad, as they often signal unmet needs, protection mechanisms, or areas calling for care. Other emotions, like joy, gratitude, love, and peace, feel light, expansive, and uplifting. These high-vibration states can open the body and mind, bringing clarity, connection, and ease. Every emotion, whether heavy or light, carries a message and an invitation to notice, understand, and respond with care. By tuning into this energetic quality, we can approach our feelings with curiosity and compassion, allowing them to guide our healing and growth.

Giving ourselves permission to feel is a profound act of self-compassion. It says, "I matter. My feelings matter. I am worthy of my own presence." Once we allow, the next step is presence—simply being with the feeling as it arises, without judgment or the need to change it. I often invite clients to notice the sensation, breathe into it, and acknowledge it as part of their story.

This doesn't mean we need to throw the door wide open all at once. At times, it may be necessary to keep it slightly ajar, especially when emotions feel intense or we sense real threats to our safety. Whether the door opens a little or more gradually, it will only open as far as the slowest, most cautious part of you that feels ready. Many of us have been conditioned to suppress or deny certain emotions, hearing messages like:

"I shouldn't feel angry."
"Sadness is a sign of weakness."
"I don't have time to deal with this right now."

Pushing emotions away doesn't make them disappear. They move deeper into the body, where they can manifest as tension, burnout, or disconnection from our true selves. Building safety first allows us to witness emotions without overwhelm, turning resistance into gentle curiosity.

I like to think of emotions as waves in the ocean: they rise, crest, and eventually ebb. Resisting them is like trying to hold back the tide; allowing them to move naturally is trusting that they will pass in their own time. Opening this door—witnessing, holding, and allowing—supports our healing journey. It teaches us to embody grace: the courage to meet ourselves fully, the gentleness to honour our emotions, and the wisdom to trust our capacity to move through life with presence and care.

Graceful Reminder

Every feeling can be witnessed with love. I don't hold on. I don't push away. I allow it to move through.

The Light that Meets the Shadow

When we give ourselves permission to truly feel, old fears and beliefs stored deep within can rise to the surface. These subconscious fears, are often what we call limiting beliefs, thoughts we have accepted as truth even though they no longer serve us.

Imagine these fears like shadows in a quiet room. At first, they might feel large and overwhelming, filling the corners of your mind. But when you turn gently towards them, allowing the light of your awareness to touch them, you begin to see their shape more clearly. They are not monsters waiting to attack, but parts of your story, messages from your past, whispers from your inner child.

These fears might whisper things like "I'm not enough" or "I don't belong." They shape how we see ourselves and the world, keeping us stuck in old patterns that no longer fit who we truly are.

When these fears come into the light, they invite us to question and transform them. This is never a quick or easy journey, but it is deeply freeing. By leaning into the feelings, meeting ourselves with grace, we open space for healing and growth.

Often, these fears show up through our behaviour without us realising. Maybe we procrastinate, avoid challenges, or conform to others to keep uncomfortable feelings at bay. Sometimes we push ourselves too hard, seek perfection, or self-sabotage to distract from what lies beneath. These reactions are unconscious attempts to protect ourselves from feeling vulnerable.

But avoiding these fears means missing out on the chance to grow. These fears are messengers. When we turn towards them gently with curiosity and kindness instead of judgement or defence, we create room for transformation.

Giving yourself permission to feel these fears expands your capacity to understand and care for yourself. What once felt like a barrier becomes a doorway to resilience and freedom.

Here are some of the dominant fears that often live beneath the surface:

Fear of Abandonment: The fear of being left alone, unloved, or unsupported by those we care about.

Fear of Failure: The fear of not meeting expectations or achieving the standards we set for ourselves or believe others have for us.

Fear of Rejection: The fear of not being accepted or valued for who we truly are.

Fear of Loss: The fear of losing what we hold dear, whether it's people, possessions, or parts of our identity.

Fear of Change: The fear of stepping into the unknown or leaving behind the comfort of the familiar.

Fear of Inadequacy: The fear of not being enough or lacking inherent worth and value.

Fear of Vulnerability: The fear of being emotionally exposed or unprotected from potential harm or pain.

Fear of Success: The fear of the responsibilities, visibility, or changes that come with achieving our goals.

Fear of Losing Control: The fear of uncertainty or being unable to influence life's events or outcomes.

Fear of Death: The fear of physical death or existential concerns about life's meaning and the unknown.

Naming these fears is a brave act. Each carries a message, inviting you to meet it with compassion and curiosity. This is how we begin to move beyond their hold and reclaim our wholeness.

Embodied Insight

As you read through the dominant fears, do any feel familiar or resonate with you? Take a moment to reflect. Which of these fears might be shaping your thoughts, behaviours, or decisions? How might they be holding you back from living in true alignment with who you really are?

The Hidden Currents of Fear

Some fears are easy to recognise. The tightness in your chest before a difficult conversation, the knot in your stomach when facing an important task, or the ache in your throat when worried someone might not approve of you. These are the fears we feel in real time, the ones we can name and notice as they arise. Other fears are more elusive. The kind that keep us awake at night without a logical reason. The ones that quietly shape our decisions, hold us back from expansion, and whisper stories about who we are and what is or is not possible. These are subconscious fears, hidden beneath the surface of our awareness, yet deeply woven into the fabric of how we live, love, and lead.

Subconscious fears are often born in moments where our nervous systems registered threat—emotional, physical, energetic, and we made an unconscious agreement to protect ourselves at all costs. They often take the form of internal beliefs like:

"If I'm too visible, I'll be judged or rejected."
"If I succeed, I'll be alone."
"If I rest, I'll be seen as lazy."
"If I speak my truth, it won't be safe."

These aren't just passing thoughts, they're imprints in the body. And they don't live in the conscious mind. They live in the subtle contraction of your shoulders when you speak up. In the flutter of your chest before you take a leap. In the tightening of your gut when you're about to receive love, support, or visibility.

For years, I carried a subconscious fear of being 'too much.' Too intuitive. Too sensitive. Too emotional. Too alive. On the surface, I appeared confident, composed, and capable. But beneath that was tension. A contraction that said, *"Hold it together. Don't make anyone uncomfortable. Be palatable. Be liked."*

It wasn't until I began attuning to the sensations in my body that I discovered I could lean into the fear rather than shrink from it. With awareness and a sense of internal safety, I could feel the tightness in my chest, the constriction in my throat, the subtle tremor in my hands and allow these sensations to be present without pushing them away. In that space, the voice of fear, fearing rejection, remembering moments when my expression was not received, or internalising the message that my full self was unsafe, could be acknowledged and met with compassion. Rather than holding myself back, I learnt to inhabit the fear, offering my body and mind the safety to explore it, to understand it, and ultimately to soften around it.

This fear didn't just affect my personal relationships. It seeped into my business, my creativity, my willingness to take up space. And like so many of my clients, I didn't even realise it was fear. I thought it was being 'realistic' or 'humble' or 'just tired.'

Subconscious fears can't be talked away. They must be felt, held, and witnessed. They arise from the subconscious because that's where the body stores unresolved moments. Times where we had to adapt to survive emotionally or energetically. These fears protect us, but they also limit us.

One of my clients, Nadia, a gentle and deeply intuitive woman, came to me feeling stuck in launching her heart-led offering. She had done the mindset work, yet her body still froze every time she spoke about her work. In our sessions, we uncovered a deeply rooted fear: If I fully show up in my truth, I will be abandoned. It traced back to an early memory of emotional disconnection when she spoke up as a child.

Together, we held that memory in her body, noticing the sinking in her belly, the tightness across her forehead, and the flutter along her spine. We did not try to fix it or push it away. Instead, we stayed present, gently turning attention to the younger Nadia who first felt this fear. Slowly, that younger self began to sense she could be safe, that she could hold herself, breathe into the tension, and soften around the fear. In that space of compassionate attention, the fear began to soften. Her body gradually released the old bracing, accompanied by small courageous movements, a deepening of her breath, a softening of her jaw, and a lightness in her pelvis. Over time, this embodied presence allowed her to reclaim her voice and step forward with more confidence, guided by a new relationship with the fear that once held her back.

The work is not to eliminate fear but to meet it with grace. To attune yourself to your body so deeply that you notice the tremble before the contraction. To offer presence before panic and choose curiosity instead of control. This is where healing becomes transformation.

Fear is not the opposite of expansion. It is the doorway to it. When met with compassion and grace, fear shows us where love wants to go next.

Your body holds ancient intelligence. It knows how to protect you and how to set you free. Subconscious fears are not blocks, they are invitations. They are parts of you longing to feel safe enough to release their grip.

And when you bring Embodied Grace to those parts through the alchemy of presence, humility, and loving action, you offer more than healing, you offer wholeness. Whether it is through breath, touch, or intuitive inquiry, this practice becomes a lived experience. Presence attunes you to what is. Humility allows you to meet it without ego or agenda. Loving action invites transformation. This is the pathway from fear to freedom, the moment where your body, heart, and soul align in grace.

This is the heart of Embodied Grace. Not bypassing fear but welcoming it as a sacred guide. Letting it reveal the places within us still longing to be seen, held, and loved into wholeness.

Embodied Insight
*What subconscious fear might be influencing your choices or holding
you back right now, even if you can't fully name it yet?*

Permission to Dream, Permission to Feel

Since I was a child, I've carried the dream of writing and publishing books. This dream lived in both the worlds of my waking imagination and my slumbering dreams. I spent countless school recesses and lunch breaks tucked away in the library, devouring fiction books and crafting stories of my own. Back then, it seemed natural that I would one day become a fiction writer, perhaps a writer of gripping crime novels.

But as the years passed and my path led me into a career in policing, my dream of being a writer seemed to fade into the background. I told myself a story, one I believed deeply at the time. "You're a police officer. That's your identity, your career, your contribution to the world."

Beneath that narrative, though, were whispers of fear. Fear of failure, fear of not being enough, fear of others' judgements. Those fears circled around me like shadows, keeping my dreams at bay.

As a police officer, writing became a different kind of act entirely. My words filled notebooks and official statements, detailing the lives and actions of myself and others. Writing became an exercise in precision, protection, and survival. Protecting the community and, in some ways, protecting myself from the community.

Journaling, which had once been a source of solace and self-expression, became too risky. I feared that my private words could someday be turned against me, that the vulnerability on those pages might be exposed. So, I stopped writing for myself.

For years, my pen was silent in the personal spaces that once felt so sacred. Without realising it, I had denied myself the permission to write freely, to feel deeply, and to express myself without fear.

One night, after a long shift, I remember quietly slipping into the house in the early hours of the morning, careful not to wake anyone. I sat in bed, restless, unable to sleep. Tossing and turning, I asked myself, "What do you need from me today?" The answer came: "Get your journal out and write." My mind resisted, frustrated by the thought of only having a few hours of sleep before the sun rose and I had to get up again. I longed for rest. But as I sat with it, my body felt a sigh of relief, a deep, calming relief that I could return to writing, that it felt safe enough to pick up the pen again.

As I wrote in my journal, my heart expanded, filled with a lightness I hadn't felt in a long time. At first, journaling felt tentative, as though I were testing the waters of my inner world. But with each word, something shifted. The layers of fear and self-doubt began to dissolve, and I realised that every word I wrote was an act of permission.

Permission to feel,
Permission to dream,
Permission to create.

As time went on something extraordinary happened. With each word, I began to celebrate myself. The more I gave myself permission to write, the more I recognised the power within me, the joy, the peace, the exhilaration. I was embracing a piece of me that had been waiting to be acknowledged. That feeling of celebration created a high vibrational state within me, a vibrance I hadn't experienced in years.

When I wrote my first book, *The Intuitive Detective*, the journey wasn't just about telling my story, it was about giving myself permission to be me. Permission to claim my dream of being a writer.

For a long time, I kept the project quiet, afraid to say it aloud. Halfway through writing the manuscript, I realised I was holding my dream at arm's length, unsure if I deserved to embrace it fully. But then, I allowed myself to speak the words, *"I am writing a book."*

Those words felt both exhilarating and terrifying. Saying them out loud wasn't just a statement, it was an act of self-acceptance, a way of allowing my emotions to surface and be acknowledged.

I allowed myself to feel the full range of high vibrational states—joy, pride, excitement, and love for myself. I was celebrating not only my writing but also the courage it took to step into my power.

Writing that book, and every moment of writing since, has been a journey of granting myself permission. Permission to feel joy, fear, vulnerability, and pride. Permission to dream and to act on those dreams. Permission to be me.

Through my journey, I have learnt that allowing ourselves to feel both high and low vibrations opens the way to deeper wisdom. Granting ourselves permission to feel creates space for our true self, and from this, our power arises. When we deny the full spectrum of emotions, we miss opportunities to heal, expand, and grow. By giving ourselves the gift of permission, we find the courage to let our emotions surface and the grace to hold them with compassion. Permission is a doorway, and allowing is the step we take through it. When we stop resisting and start allowing, we realise that the dreams we once thought impossible were always within reach, and in that allowance, we find a deep and radiant celebration of our whole selves, embracing all our vibrational states.

Embodied Insight

What dream have you been holding at arm's length?
Explore what fears, stories, or emotions might be keeping it at bay.
Then, ask yourself:
What permission do I need to give myself today to take one step closer
to that dream?
Let your words be an act of celebration, an embrace of all that you
feel, and a declaration of who you are becoming.

Seeing Yourself on the Page

Have you ever written something down and suddenly felt lighter?
Like you were finally heard, even if it was only by yourself?

Journaling is a powerful practice that can support you at any point in this journey, but I've placed it here with intention, because it offers something profound: permission.

Permission to tell the truth.
To name what has been unspoken.
To witness your emotions and subconscious fears on the page, instead of carrying them silently within.

When I began journaling, I wasn't sure what would come out. Sometimes, it was messy. Sometimes, it was random, scattered thoughts, half-formed feelings, even just lists of words. But every time, it was real. And it helped me meet parts of myself I didn't even know were waiting.

One of my clients once shared that journaling felt awkward at first, like she was writing to no one. But after a few days, she wrote something that made her cry. Not because it was painful, but because it was true. She said, "I think I finally heard myself for the first time."

That's the power of being witnessed by your own heart.

When you put pen to paper, you create space for clarity, curiosity, and compassion. You allow more of the 8 Cs to emerge in your awareness. Through journaling, all parts of you begin to feel safe enough to come forward, express their truth, and release what has been held inside for too long.

You don't have to write anything perfect. This isn't about grammar or getting it 'right.' It's about presence. It's about choosing to show up, even if all you can write is, "I don't know where to start." That's a start too.

This process is an act of Embodied Grace. It teaches you to meet yourself where you are, without judgement. As you write, you soften the edges of self-criticism and make space for self-compassion. You begin to honour your emotions rather than resist them. You learn to listen with kindness, creating a bridge between your inner world and the safety your nervous system craves.

Journaling allows you to be fully seen, by you. It's a practice of deep self-witnessing. A way to create and hold space for your own healing. A step toward embodying grace in every part of your life.

Let this be your permission slip.

Find a quiet moment, pick up your pen, and let whatever wants to be expressed flow through.
You are safe to be seen, especially by yourself.
There's no need to rush. Let your pen be an anchor as you begin to gently explore what's stirring beneath the surface.
What emotions are ready to be witnessed?
What truths are waiting to be named?

The following journaling practice invites you to meet yourself in this tender space, with curiosity, with compassion, and with courage. You're not alone in this. You're held—by your breath, by the page, and by the wisdom rising from within.

Practice: Writing with Grace

Find a quiet, comfortable place. Have your journal and pen ready. Set a timer for 5 minutes.

Invite your eyes to gently close if it feels safe, or soften your gaze. Breathe in slowly through your nose, and exhale with a releasing sigh. Let each breath guide you into presence and ease in your body.

Place your hand on your heart. Feel the connection, letting your breath deepen and your mind settle.

Silently or aloud, say: "I allow myself to be fully seen on this page. I write with honesty, curiosity, and grace."

When you feel ready, gently open your eyes and place your pen on the page. Write, "What do you want me to know?" Let your body, heart, or intuition answer. Allow words to flow naturally, without judgement.

Remember, you don't need full sentences. You can start with dot points, jotting down feelings, images, or fragments of thought. Engage all your senses as you write. Over time, those dot points and feelings come together. A sentence forms, then a paragraph, a page, a chapter—and before you know it, a whole book.

If you're unsure what your heart wants to share, you could try one of these prompts and see where it leads you:

- *What truth is ready to be witnessed today?*

- *How can I offer myself more grace in this moment?*

- *What emotions have I been holding onto, and what would they say if I gave them space to speak?*

- *If my heart could write me a letter, what would it say?*

When the timer goes off, pause. Place your hand on your heart and acknowledge yourself for showing up. Whisper or write a note of gratitude: "Thank you for listening. Thank you for honouring me." When you feel ready, gently open your eyes fully and return your attention to the room around you.

Wandering at the Edges

Throughout my life, I've often found myself hovering at the edges of connection. Close enough to witness belonging, yet never fully inside the circle. This feeling wasn't sudden. It settled in early and quietly stayed with me through my tweens, teens, and into adulthood. No matter the setting, school, work, or social gatherings, there was a recurring sense of standing just outside the warmth of the group.

I remember being in my tweens, sitting in the schoolyard watching classmates laugh together in their tight-knit groups. There was a quiet ache in my chest, a longing to be part of something I couldn't quite reach. I'd retreat to the library, finding comfort in books where I could momentarily imagine myself woven into other worlds. I wasn't without friends, and I was included now and then, an invite to a party, a spot in a conversation, but those moments always felt like exceptions, not the usual. Like I was welcome enough to be nearby, but never truly known.

For years, I didn't acknowledge it. I just assumed it was a part of life, something to deal with. As time went on, I realised what I was really avoiding were my emotions and the subconscious fears that were beneath it. I was terrified of feeling the weight of exclusion, of not being enough. So, I ignored it, buried it beneath layers of striving for approval and acceptance. But, in truth, all I was doing was prolonging the pain.

When my son was diagnosed with ADHD and Autism, this feeling took on a new layer. There were times when he wouldn't be invited to birthday parties, but his twin sister was. It was heartbreaking to witness, as I could see the other children's bonds forming while he found it challenging to fit in. Starting kindergarten was especially challenging for him, and there were many moments when he would throw a chair or a table in class. The fear of judgement loomed large for me as I watched how others responded to his behaviour. When I would have meetings with the school, we were told constantly how other parents were making complaints of our son and his meltdowns in class as it was disruptive. This fuelled into my subconscious fears of being judged.

When he was invited to parties, I still found myself standing back, unsure of how I would be received. I carried the weight of judgement, fearing that others were already forming opinions about me as a mother, about him as a child. This fear was deeply tied to my experiences of exclusion, and it fuelled the cycle of feeling abandoned. I had a tendency to hold myself back in those situations, thinking I wasn't enough, or that my family wasn't enough to be embraced as part of the group.

When I began to witness my emotions more truthfully, clarity emerged. I realised that I had spent so much time avoiding this feeling, fearing it meant I was unworthy or unloved, that I had never truly allowed myself to feel it.

When we open ourselves to our emotions, fear can surface. Fear of vulnerability, fear of the unknown, fear of being overwhelmed. But alongside fear lies the possibility of love, the love that rises when we honour ourselves enough to feel.

Marianne Williamson shares in her book *A Return to Love,*[15]

> *"Our defenses reflect our wounds. But*
> *no person can heal those wounds. They*
> *can give us love, innocently and sincerely,*
> *but if we're already convinced that people*
> *can't be trusted—if that's the decision*
> *we've already made—then our mind will*
> *construe whatever someone's behavior is,*
> *as evidence that our previously drawn*
> *conclusion was correct."*

This quote struck me because it perfectly reflected how I had been living. I had created defences, walls, and fears based on past wounds, and I had convinced myself that people couldn't be trusted to truly accept me for who I was. I was caught in a cycle of projecting my insecurities and past hurts onto others, without ever truly letting anyone in. The fear of rejection. Of not being enough, had caused me to build these invisible barriers, shutting out the very connections I longed for. I'd often find myself pulling away or staying in the background, convinced that I wasn't welcome or that I wouldn't be accepted.

I realised that I had been living as though I wasn't deserving of love or connection. I had been waiting for others to show me that I belonged, without first showing myself that I was enough. This realisation was eye-opening. I had unknowingly been pushing people away, creating a space where I always felt 'on the outside,' because deep down, I believed that's where I belonged.

When I feared being alone, I built walls around myself, thinking they would protect me from hurt and rejection. But in truth, these walls only made me feel more isolated and abandoned. It was a paradox. I created separation to avoid pain, but the very walls I built to shield myself only deepened my sense of isolation. This pattern repeated itself throughout my life. Whenever I felt alone, rather than facing my fear and vulnerability, I retreated and reinforced those walls, unintentionally distancing myself further from connection and love.

I wanted to change this pattern. At the next children's birthday party we attended, I considered standing in the corner for the duration of the event. Before I even got out of the car, I took a moment to reflect and asked myself, "Is this choice coming from love or fear?" The answer came through intuitively—fear. And I knew that meant it was time for change.

As I navigated these emotions, I realised that it was okay to explore different friendships and connections. I started engaging in conversations with people, including other parents at school, and something beautiful began to unfold. I met parents with neurodivergent children who offered guidance and understanding, having walked a similar path years earlier. Some parents even asked for my advice as they navigated getting their children assessed, while others simply offered compassion. Not every interaction resulted in rejection or judgement. Many were filled with understanding. And most of all, the way the parents spoke of my son was filled with nothing but love.

This didn't mean I had to open my heart to everyone. I didn't need to force myself into every circle or place where I wasn't fully embraced. Opening my heart to the possibility of connection—without the pressure to fit in—gave me the freedom to discover the spaces where I truly belonged. It wasn't about being everywhere or with everyone. It was about finding the places where my true self could be seen and received with love.

This journey was slow, but it ultimately led me to a place of peace with myself. I stopped running from the feeling of being left out and instead learnt to embrace myself with compassion. I recognised my wound, not as something that defined me, but as a part of my past that was ready for healing. Through this process, I stopped searching for validation from others and began to cultivate a sense of belonging from within. I allowed myself to fully feel and honour my emotions, no longer fearing what they might reveal. Here I embodied grace.

Witnessing my emotions in this way shifted my perspective where I discovered a new path to self-love and acceptance. I stepped into a space of radical self-compassion, no longer fearing being alone because I had learnt to be with myself, in all my imperfect beauty. This clarity allowed me to release layers of the fear of rejection and abandonment, opening the door to authentic connections and deep, loving relationships. First with myself, and then with others.

Graceful Reminder
Grace begins when we stop waiting for the world to embrace us and start embracing ourselves. In that radical acceptance, we open the door to love, connection, and the courage to stand fully seen.

The Cricket Game

My husband, Grant, is a devoted cricket fan. Not only does he love watching the game, but he's also quite the player himself. Before we had children, he even travelled to England two years in a row to play cricket for clubs. If you're not familiar with the game, cricket matches can last for hours, and Grant often finds ways to stay connected to the sport. He listens to games on his phone while doing things around the house, watches matches or highlights in the background, and later, when he wants to rest, will lie on the bed and continue following the game.

One evening, I saw him lying on the bed, phone in hand, watching cricket. A surge of frustration and anger rose within me. My chest tightened, a heaviness settled in my stomach, and my shoulders tensed almost involuntarily. My jaw clenched, my hands curled slightly, and I felt heat rising through my face as my nervous system shifted into a dysregulated sympathetic state. I found myself becoming passive-aggressive, making sharp comments or sighing heavily as if to make my feelings known without directly saying a word.

This pattern continued for a month, and each time I saw him lying on the bed watching cricket, my anger intensified. Then, one afternoon, when I was on the verge of snapping, I caught myself. Instead of letting the anger take over, I stepped outside, sat on the grass, and connected with the earth. I used the grounding energy of nature as a resource for safety within my nervous system. I gave myself permission to feel the anger fully, not to suppress or dismiss it, but to truly witness it within my heart.

As I sat there, I gently asked myself, What's beneath this anger? What fear is hidden underneath?

What surfaced surprised me. Beneath the anger was worry, and beneath that worry was an old, familiar fear, the fear of being abandoned. At first, I was confused. How could this moment, this seemingly small frustration about cricket, be tied to abandonment?

Later that night, as I lay in bed, it hit me, an *aha* moment of clarity. My fear of abandonment was tied to my dad. Memories came flooding back of him lying in bed, lost in his music, the stereo playing softly in the background. These moments from my childhood became entwined with the pain of his death by suicide, a loss that left me grappling with the belief that I could be left behind at any moment.

And here was my nervous system, decades later, replaying that fear. Even though I understood logically that Grant wasn't on the bed watching cricket because he was depressed or planning to leave, my body responded as if it were. My nervous system couldn't distinguish between the past and the present, it only knew the familiar echoes of abandonment.

As I became aware, something shifted within me. I realised that my anger wasn't a flaw or a failure. It was a messenger. It was my body's way of alerting me to a deeper wound that needed my attention. By leaning into the discomfort, asking questions, and holding space for myself with compassion, I began to embody grace.

Grace showed up as understanding, not just of the fear itself but of the tender parts of me that had carried this fear for so long. It showed up as forgiveness, both for myself and for Grant, who had unknowingly become the mirror reflecting my old wounds. And it showed up as love, the kind of love that reminds us we are whole, even with our imperfections and pain.

Practice: Meeting Fear with Grace

Gently close your eyes if it feels safe, or soften your gaze. Take a slow, deep inhale through your nose, and exhale with an audible sigh. Let each exhale be slightly longer than your inhale, inviting release.

Bring your awareness to any stress, tension, discomfort, or lingering patterns in your body. Allow whatever arises without judgment. Notice where this sensation lives—is it heavy or light, tight or open, still or moving? Attend to its texture, temperature, or tone without trying to change it.

Place your hand over your heart. Keep your breath steady and deep. Let this gentle touch signal to your nervous system: "I am safe. I am here. I am held."

Feel your breath, your body, and the subtle vibration within you. Notice tingling, warmth, stillness, or simply awareness. Let this vibration expand with each breath.

Gently ask yourself: "What fear is present here?" Allow whatever arises—word, image, or bodily sensation—to be present. Breathe with it, giving it space in your body, holding it with curiosity and compassion.

Once the fear is acknowledged, bring to mind a memory or feeling of joy, freedom, appreciation, or love. Allow it to gently meet the area where the fear lives. Let it expand with your breath, flowing alongside the fear, softening tension, and creating room for both sensations to coexist. Breathe into this space for 2–3 minutes, noticing subtle shifts—more softness, stillness, and spaciousness in your body.

Take a final deep breath in and exhale with an audible sigh. Gently move your body—wiggle your fingers, rotate your shoulders, stretch. When ready, softly open your eyes and return to the room, carrying this sense of embodied presence, compassion, and balance with you.

The Depths Within

Beautiful soul,

Beneath the surface of your thoughts, beneath the surface of your daily life, lies a vast ocean of emotions, fears, and untold stories. The layers you wear to protect yourself are real, but they are not your truth. They are simply veils, created out of fear and conditioned responses, but they do not define who you truly are.

The emotions you feel, whether joy or sorrow, anger or peace, are like currents in that ocean. They are fluid, ever-moving, and ever-shifting. When you take a moment to witness these emotions, to allow them to rise and fall without judgement, you begin to uncover the truths they hold. These emotions are messengers, guiding you to deeper understandings that have long been hidden in the shadows of your heart.

But it is not enough to simply witness them. You must hold them with grace. With each wave of emotion that comes, you are invited to meet it with compassion, not resistance. The fear beneath the surface, the fear of feeling too much or being overwhelmed, is but an illusion. You are not here to suppress or avoid. You are here to feel fully, to be present with what arises, and to honour it as part of your journey.

In witnessing and holding your emotions with grace, you begin to build trust within yourself. You start to understand that you are capable of navigating even the deepest waters of your

OWN HEART. YOU BEGIN TO KNOW, DEEP WITHIN, THAT THERE IS NOTHING THAT YOU CANNOT FACE. YOU ARE STRONGER THAN YOU REALISE, MORE RESILIENT THAN YOU'VE GIVEN YOURSELF CREDIT FOR.

AS YOU MOVE THROUGH THIS PROCESS OF SELF-WITNESSING, OF HOLDING YOURSELF WITH TENDERNESS, THE FEAR BEGINS TO LOOSEN ITS GRIP. IT IS THROUGH THIS ACCEPTANCE THAT TRUE HEALING OCCURS. IN HEALING, YOU EXPAND. YOU EXPAND INTO THE FULLNESS OF YOUR BEING, INTO THE BRILLIANCE THAT HAS ALWAYS BEEN WITHIN YOU, BUT WAS CLOUDED BY DOUBT AND DISCONNECTION.

TRUST YOURSELF, DEAR ONE. TRUST THAT THE JOURNEY BENEATH THE SURFACE IS ONE OF DEEP TRANSFORMATION. EACH MOMENT OF GRACE, EACH STEP OF HEALING, LEADS YOU CLOSER TO THE RADIANT BEING YOU ARE MEANT TO BE. EMBRACE THIS JOURNEY WITH LOVE AND PATIENCE, KNOWING THAT AS YOU HOLD YOURSELF WITH GRACE, YOU OPEN THE DOORS TO THE TRUST, HEALING, AND EXPANSION THAT AWAIT YOU.

YOU ARE ON THE PATH OF REMEMBERING YOUR WHOLENESS. STEP FORWARD WITH COURAGE, AND KNOW THAT YOU ARE SUPPORTED BY THE DEEPEST WISDOM OF YOUR BEING.

PART SEVEN

Shedding the Burden of Shame

The Shape Shame Takes

There are moments when shame does not announce itself. It lingers quietly in the hesitation before we speak, in the shrinking of our body, in the apology that comes too quickly. It becomes a familiar undertone in our lives, hidden beneath smiles, perfectionism, and overachievement. It whispers that we are too much or not enough or somehow both.

For many of us, this begins early. We learn to tuck parts of ourselves away to belong, to stay safe, to be loved. Over time, those messages root themselves deep within. We carry them not as passing thoughts but as truths about who we are. This is the insidious nature of shame. It embeds itself silently until it shapes how we see ourselves and the world.

Among the eight core human emotions, five are considered survival based: fear, disgust, shame, anger, and sadness.[16] These emotions activate cortisol, the body's primary stress hormone, and are closely linked to self-protection. Shame, in particular, is quiet yet potent, embedding itself deep within the body. Often these emotions move beneath our awareness, guiding our choices and shaping our patterns without conscious intent.

For women, shame is often entangled with patriarchy. Many of us have been conditioned to shrink, stay quiet, and avoid taking up space. Often this silence is a survival response, shaped by real or perceived consequences. When we do not speak up, a quiet shame settles in, becoming default. Subtle, but powerful.

If you are a woman in today's world, you have felt this in some form. You may not yet name it for what it was, but you have carried it. This shame leaves an imprint, often unspoken. But awareness loosens its grip.

For me, shame was already familiar by the time I reached high school, a place where belonging felt like a survival skill. I remember the knot in my stomach as I walked into classrooms, my natural red hair drawing more stares than smiles. Some kids teased me, calling me names and making me feel too loud, too different, too visible. Others left me on the sidelines with quiet exclusion, watching as fitting in seemed effortless for everyone else. I learnt to stay quiet, to shrink away from attention, and to hide parts of myself that did not fit the norm. I hesitated to speak up, afraid my words would only bring more teasing or rejection. That silence was more than fear. It was shame settling in, whispering that my true self was not enough, that I needed to change to be accepted or loved. Looking back, I see how deeply that shame shaped how I moved through the world for years, keeping me small and cautious. But I also see how those shadows can soften, and grace can help us find courage to step fully into our true colours.

As a parent to a neurodivergent child, I have witnessed how shame can settle silently in their heart. Many neurodivergent individuals receive the message, directly or indirectly, that their way of being is wrong or less than. This shame may not be obvious, but it shows up in hesitation before speaking, retreating inward, or doubting themselves when misunderstood.

In a world that values sameness, both neurodivergent and neurotypical people can internalise the belief they need to hide who they truly are. The pressure to conform becomes exhausting. Over time, this shame shapes their sense of self. But shame is not your truth. It does not define you. Beneath it lies something far more powerful—grace.

Grace invites us to meet these hidden parts of ourselves with compassion rather than judgement. It creates a soft space where we can acknowledge shame without letting it dictate our worth. We begin to see shame not as a flaw, but as a learnt response, one that can be softened and released.

Through grace, we remember that our worth is not conditional. It is not about being good enough for others. It is rooted in our humanity and the kindness we extend to ourselves.

As you practice this, you will find that releasing shame is essential to healing. Shame keeps us small. It holds us back from fully engaging with life. As you shed its layers, we reclaim our right to live authentically, free from self-condemnation. Grace reminds us that healing is not about perfection. It is about presence, tenderness, and choosing to honour yourself as you are.

I think back to that teenage girl. The one who kept her head down in the classroom, who muted her voice to avoid being noticed, who quietly believed that who she was would never be enough. I no longer silence her. Through grace, I have learnt to sit with her gently, to let her know she never had to change to be worthy. She did not need to be quieter, smaller, or less herself. I honour her now. Not by pretending the shame never existed, but by no longer letting it define who I am.

Honouring her has shown me what it truly means to live from grace.

This shift changes everything. It transforms how we relate to ourself and lays the foundation for kindness in every part of our life.

The importance of this cannot be overstated. Releasing shame opens the way to self-compassion, resilience, and a deeper sense of self. It frees us to step into our wholeness, where our worth is no longer bound by conditions but held in the compassionate truth of who we are. Through grace, we return to ourself. Rooted in kindness. Aligned in authenticity. Ready to live with freedom and joy.

Graceful Reminder

Releasing shame is not about changing who you are, but about unburdening yourself from the weight of false beliefs. In the space where shame once resided, grace blooms, reminding you of your inherent worth and inviting you to live from a place of authentic power.

The Many Faces of Shame

Shame is like a shadow that lingers in the corners of our being, whispering stories of inadequacy, failure, and disconnection. It's a feeling we've all encountered, whether briefly or as a recurring presence, shaping the way we see ourselves and the world. But shame isn't a single entity. It's a complex and multi-layered experience that can show up in many forms. Each layer carries its own weight, shaped by our personal experiences, our culture, our relationships, and even our spiritual beliefs. Understanding these faces of shame allows us to navigate them with greater awareness, compassion, and, ultimately, freedom.

To better understand how shame manifests and influences our lives, it's important to look at the different types of shame that we may carry.

Personal Shame

Personal shame often grows from our individual experiences. It may stem from a single moment, like a harsh word that cut too deep, or a series of events that made us feel less than enough. These moments create internal narratives: "I'm not good enough," "I'm unworthy," or "I'll never measure up." Left unchecked, these stories become the lens through which we view ourselves. But in reality, personal shame is never the full story. It's a fragment, a perspective shaped by circumstance, not an unchanging fact about who we are.

Cultural Shame

Our culture plays a significant role in shaping our sense of worth. From an early age, we're bombarded with messages about what it means to be 'beautiful,' 'successful,' or 'worthy.' These ideals are often unattainable and worse, deeply narrow. When we don't fit into these moulds, shame creeps in, whispering, "You're not enough." But cultural shame isn't a reflection of our truth. It's a byproduct of external pressures that often have nothing to do with our inherent worth.

Generational Shame

Have you ever felt a sense of shame that you couldn't quite place? Perhaps it's an inherited burden, passed down through generations. Our ancestors' unspoken traumas, fears, and losses can become embedded in our family stories and, by extension, in us. Generational shame reminds us of the interconnectedness of our healing. When we face and release this layer, we not only free ourselves but also pave the way for future generations to live with more ease and joy.

Body Shame

Our relationship with our body is deeply personal, yet it's also shaped by societal standards and external judgement. Body shame can manifest as criticism of our appearance, discomfort in our skin, or disconnection from our physical selves. It's the voice that says, "You're too much," or "You're not enough." Reclaiming our relationship with our body involves listening to its wisdom, honouring its needs, and recognising it as a sacred vessel for our experiences and growth.

Relational Shame

Relationships hold immense power to either nurture or wound us. Relational shame arises when we feel unworthy of love, connection, or belonging. It often stems from past hurts, a betrayal, a rejection, or a lack of validation. This shame convinces us that we're too flawed to be truly seen and loved. But the truth is, our worth isn't defined by others. It's intrinsic, woven into the very fabric of our being.

Moral Shame

Moral shame appears when we feel we've failed to live up to our values or ethical standards. It can be a powerful force for reflection and growth, but when it turns into self-condemnation, it becomes destructive. Instead of seeing our mistakes as opportunities to learn, we might label ourselves as 'wrong' or 'bad.' Healing this layer involves recognising the difference between guilt (what I've done) and shame (who I am) and allowing self-compassion to guide us back to alignment.

Spiritual Shame

At its core, spiritual shame is a disconnection from our sacred essence. It can arise from feeling unworthy of divine love, forgiveness, or connection to a higher power. For those who've experienced spiritual trauma or dogmatic beliefs, this layer can feel particularly heavy. Yet, spiritual shame also holds an invitation—to reconnect with the divine within us, to redefine our spiritual path, and to trust that we are already whole, already loved.

Shame of Vulnerability

To be vulnerable is to be human. Yet, for many, vulnerability feels synonymous with weakness. The shame of vulnerability tells us it's not safe to be seen, to share our truth, or to ask for support. It's the armour we wear to protect ourselves from judgement or rejection. But true strength lies in our willingness to be real, to let others witness our authentic selves, and to embrace the beauty of our shared humanity.

Shame of Success or Joy

This layer often hides in plain sight. The shame of success or joy whispers that we don't deserve to thrive, that our accomplishments might alienate others, or that happiness will be fleeting. It's closely tied to imposter syndrome and survivor's guilt. Releasing this shame means allowing ourselves to celebrate our wins, to revel in joy, and to trust that we are worthy of all the good life offers.

Internalised Shame

Perhaps the deepest layer, internalised shame becomes part of our identity. It's the persistent belief that there is something fundamentally wrong with us. This layer often feels the hardest to face, but it's also where the greatest transformation can occur. By turning inward with curiosity and compassion, we can begin to unravel these deeply held beliefs and remember the sacred truth: we are enough, just as we are.

I don't know about you, but I can relate to each part of these faces of shame. In my journey, I've experienced moments of personal shame that have shaped my self-worth, moments when I've internalised cultural expectations and tried to fit into moulds that never quite felt right. There have been times I've felt disconnected from my body or wondered if I was worthy of love or belonging. I've carried the weight of generational shame without even realising it, and I've struggled with the moral shame of feeling like I wasn't living up to my values. And, perhaps most intimately, I've had moments of spiritual shame, where I've questioned my worthiness in the eyes of the divine.

The reality is that these faces aren't isolated from one another. They intertwine, sometimes overlapping in subtle ways, and they leave their imprint on how we show up in the world. It's through recognising and understanding these faces of shame that we begin to dismantle the stories we've been carrying, so we can heal and reconnect with our true selves. I invite you to reflect on how these faces of shame might show up in your life, and to approach them with gentleness and curiosity.

Understanding the faces of shame is not about dissecting ourselves or assigning blame. It's about bringing light to the places within us that have been shrouded in misunderstanding and fear. By turning inward with curiosity and tenderness, we begin to soften those dimensions, honouring each one as part of our story while remembering it doesn't define who we are.

By reconnecting with our body, we access the wisdom it holds about our shame and our healing. Through self-compassion, we soften the edges of self-judgement and create space for transformation. And by trusting in our intuitive knowing, we open ourselves to the guidance of something greater. The divine truth that we are whole, worthy, and loved.

As we release the faces of shame within, the 8 Cs: Calmness, Curiosity, Clarity, Compassion, Confidence, Creativity, Courage, and Connectedness (as shared in Part 3) naturally begin to emerge. We might notice a sense of calm settling in our chest, curiosity bubbling up as we explore new possibilities, or clarity washing over our mind. Compassion may soften our inner dialogue, confidence may strengthen our posture, or creativity may stir within. These shifts often manifest in the body as gentle warmth in the heart, lightness in the limbs, or a grounding sensation through the feet.

The journey through the faces of shame is not linear or rushed. It's a tender process of coming home to ourselves, one breath, one insight, one act of kindness at a time. And with each layer we release, we make room for grace, joy, and connection to flow more freely through our lives.

Embodied Insight

Which face/s of shame feels most present in your life right now, and in what ways has it influenced your relationship with yourself and others?

Shame Held in My Heart

As I opened my eyes, a sharp, throbbing pain shot through my head. An all-too-familiar hangover from too much alcohol and too little care for myself. Blinking against the morning light, I tried to focus, but the room was completely unfamiliar. Panic surged through me. *Where am I?*

I bolted upright, realising I was lying on a couch in someone's living room. Slowly, the fragmented memories of the previous night began to piece themselves together.

The Christmas after-party. Still wearing my outfit from the night before. My stomach dropped as I reached for my phone. Missed calls. Dozens of messages. All from Grant. I was supposed to have only had a couple of drinks and catch the last train home.

Heart pounding, I called him, stumbling through apologies. "I'm so sorry," I croaked, my voice raw and shaky. "I passed out... I drank too much." Saying the words out loud felt like pouring cold water over myself. The truth stung, settling heavily in my chest.

The evening had started innocently enough, the annual Christmas party for the police station where I worked as a detective. Dinner was beautiful, filled with lively chatter and alcohol. But when we moved to a colleague's house for the after-party, things spiralled. What seemed like a harmless continuation of the celebration turned into something far more when I surrendered myself to the haze of alcohol.

But it wasn't just the festive spirit that drove me to drink that night. Beneath it all, I was carrying a wound so deep I hadn't even acknowledged it. The day before had been the anniversary of my father's death, a loss that still felt raw, even after two decades. I had done my usual routine of regulation tools, ticking boxes as if to manage my emotions, but I had avoided the day's weight entirely. I bypassed my grief, distracting myself until it bubbled over in the only way it knew how, a desperate attempt to numb the pain.

And here I was, hungover and disoriented, searching my phone's Maps app to tell Grant where to pick me up. When he arrived, he was calm and steady, bringing with him various drinks, including water, electrolytes, and soft drink, along with paracetamol in case I needed them. He didn't berate me. He didn't scold or shame me. His support should have been comforting, but it became a mirror reflecting my shame back at me.

That shame was suffocating. It settled like a heavy weight in my chest, gripping tightly at my shoulders, churning in my stomach, and aching in my heart. My mind replayed the night in relentless detail, filling in the blanks with harsh self-judgement. Friends shared parts of the night I couldn't remember, moments where I yelled at people, cried inconsolably that I was alone and had no friends, and passed out on the grass in the front yard. Their accounts stung deeply, each one chipping away at my self-esteem.

Going into work for my next shift felt impossible. Thoughts of what my colleagues must think of me consumed me. My embarrassment turned inward, feeding the ever-growing shame narrative I'd carried for years. I knew I couldn't move forward until I faced this shame and unravelled its hold on me.

It wasn't easy. Sitting with the shame meant fully feeling it, letting it exist without pushing it away. It was raw, uncomfortable, and confronting. But it was also the beginning of something else, honesty. For the first time, I could see my shame not as a punishment but as a guide, pointing me towards the parts of myself that needed compassion.

I recognised that the day before, I hadn't truly acknowledged the anniversary of my dad's death. I had done everything to avoid feeling the sadness, the grief, the deep sense of abandonment. I had bypassed my emotions entirely, telling myself I was fine when I wasn't.

Through this process, I began to unpack the shame narrative that had taken root within me. It was a story of harsh self-judgement, avoidance, and unworthiness, a belief that I was failing, not just in my actions but as a person. I saw myself as someone who didn't deserve compassion, even when Grant offered it so freely, and I felt an overwhelming need to suppress my emotions, to bypass grief and vulnerability rather than face them.

This narrative isolated me, convincing me that my pain was mine alone to carry and that my actions defined me in the eyes of others. Every misstep felt like proof of my inadequacy. But as I sat with the discomfort of these feelings, I began to uncover the truth. My shame wasn't a punishment, it was a signal, a guide pointing toward the parts of me that needed care and compassion. Slowly, I started dismantling the lies within this narrative, replacing them with a more honest and loving understanding of myself. My grief and emotions were no longer things to avoid but invitations to heal, to hold myself with the tenderness I had long denied.

Gradually, I felt a shift. The shame didn't vanish overnight, but its grip began to loosen. In its place, I discovered understanding, compassion, forgiveness, and grace.

I realised my heart wasn't merely a container for shame, it was the birthplace of healing. By holding space for my shadow, I gave myself permission to step into the light. It wasn't about striving for perfection or pretending the pain didn't exist. It was about meeting myself where I was, with kindness and compassion, and choosing to let the healing begin.

Practice: Softening the Grip of Shame

Find a comfortable seated or lying position. Close your eyes if it feels safe. Take a few deep, slow breaths. With each inhale, let your body expand. With each exhale, soften into the support beneath you. Feel grounded and safe.

Rest your hands on your chest, thighs, or the ground. Notice the connection and let it deepen with your breath.

Slowly scan from head to toe. Notice tension, tightness, or heaviness. Gently ask, "Where do I feel shame in my body?" Simply notice without trying to change anything.

When you locate an area of shame, place your hands softly there. Take a few steady breaths into that space, breathing in warmth and compassion.

Ask, "What thought, belief, or memory lives here?" Notice what arises without judgement. You are simply listening, not analysing.

Quietly say to the sensation, "I see you. I honour you. I hold space for you." Imagine the discomfort softening with each exhale, like mist lifting from water.

With each breath, visualise the heaviness leaving your body, absorbed gently into the earth. Imagine a warm, golden light filling the space, spreading through your body like a balm. Let it soothe, calm, and remind you: you are safe, whole, and enough.

Take a few grounding breaths. Wiggle your fingers and toes. Bring awareness back to the room around you.

Notice any shifts in sensation. Consider journaling what came up. Over time, this practice helps you meet shame with compassion and deepen self-acceptance.

The Weight of Burdening Shame

Shame is one of the most insidious emotions we can carry. Unlike guilt, which focuses on specific actions, shame seeps deep into our identity, telling us that there is something inherently wrong with who we are. It whispers that we're not enough, and we don't deserve the love, success, or peace others might have. And when left unchecked, it can become a heavy burden that shapes how we show up in the world.

Shame often takes root in our early experiences, messages from others or ourselves that tell us we are unworthy or flawed. I remember a client, Abigail, who came to me with a deep sense of shame rooted in her childhood. Growing up in a family where 'achievement' was a measure of worth, any sign of failure was met with harsh criticism. Abigail recalled one incident in school when she received a grade lower than expected and her father's disapproving silence spoke louder than words. That silence told her she was a failure, a belief that stuck with her well into adulthood.

Similarly, I've experienced moments in my life that planted the seeds of shame. I was constantly striving for perfection whether in my work, relationships, or personal life and any perceived failure made me feel like I wasn't enough. The voice of shame would remind me that I didn't measure up. I had to do more and be more, just to be accepted or loved.

For Abigail, these early seeds grew into a belief that she was never good enough. Even when she earned promotions at work, she couldn't shake the thought that she had somehow tricked others into thinking she was competent. She would wait for the 'inevitable' moment when someone would realise she wasn't worthy. Shame kept her in a cycle of overcompensation, doing everything perfectly but never feeling like she truly belonged. She had convinced herself that her worth was tied to how others saw her, rather than her intrinsic value.

The weight of shame doesn't always look like tears or visible struggle. In fact, it can manifest as something far quieter: an internal dialogue of self-doubt, a tendency to overcompensate, or an ever-present sense of fear that you will be found out. Many of my clients struggle with this quietly for years. On the outside, they appear confident and successful, but internally, they battle a constant fear of being exposed as a fraud. No matter what achievements they reach, they always feel like an imposter. The thought of someone seeing through them—seeing that they weren't perfec—would send them into spirals of anxiety.

In my life, this burden of shame appeared as perfectionism. I had to get everything right. Every speech, every interaction, every task. I thought if I were perfect, I would finally feel worthy of love and success. But this only led to burnout. Even when I succeeded, I was too focused on the next thing to allow myself to truly celebrate or appreciate what I had achieved.

This was a common theme for many of the clients I worked with, people who could never sit in the peace of their accomplishments because they felt they were never enough. In their eyes, any mistake or imperfection was proof that they weren't deserving of what they had earned. The voice of shame lingered, always telling them they were 'too much' or 'not enough' at the same time, creating a constant internal tug-of-war.

To release the burden of shame, we must first become aware of it. Shame thrives in secrecy, in the dark corners of our minds where we hide our perceived flaws. By bringing it into the light, by acknowledging and naming it, we can begin to understand it. With Abigail, the breakthrough moment came when she realised that she was still holding on to the shame of her childhood, allowing it to dictate her worth. In our work together, we explored how her self-criticism was not rooted in her true self but in external expectations. The act of naming her shame allowed her to separate her worth from the opinions of others. It was a pivotal step in beginning her healing process.

For me, the shift came when I finally admitted to myself that I wasn't perfect and that was okay. I didn't have to be everything to everyone. The pressure I had been placing on myself was suffocating, and by releasing the need to be flawless, I made room for self-compassion.

Shame often tells us that we are alone in our struggles, that we are the only ones who feel unworthy. But the truth is, everyone carries some form of shame. We are not as isolated in our pain as we might believe. One of my clients, Winnie, shared that she felt ashamed of her past mistakes, particularly when it came to her relationships. But when she began to open up in our sessions, she realised that so many of us carry similar stories. Stories of imperfection, vulnerability, and growth. This shared experience created space for healing and understanding.

Forgiveness is an essential part of releasing the burden of shame. It starts with forgiving ourselves for the things we did or didn't do, for the mistakes we made, for the times we thought we weren't enough. With Abigail, we focused on self-forgiveness and how it could break the cycle of self-judgement that had kept her stuck. She had spent years trying to prove she was worthy, but by forgiving herself for her perceived shortcomings, she began to feel lighter, freer. It wasn't about excusing the mistakes she had made. It was about giving herself permission to be human.

When I worked on forgiving myself, it felt like lifting a weight I hadn't even realised I was carrying. Every time I forgave myself for past mistakes or imperfections, I allowed myself to embrace my humanity. I wasn't 'perfect' but I was enough.

To release the burden of shame, we must also rewrite the narrative we've been carrying. Instead of seeing ourselves as broken or unworthy, we can choose to see ourselves as resilient, capable, and deserving of love and success. For Abigail, this meant learning to recognise that her achievements were hers, not handed to her by anyone else's validation. She started reframing her life through a lens of empowerment: *I am capable. I am worthy.* This shift helped her embrace her true worth and stop apologising for simply being herself.

Releasing shame also involves embracing our authentic selves, the parts of us that we've hidden out of fear of judgement or rejection. When we let go of shame, we give ourselves permission to show up as we truly are, without the need for perfection or approval from others. This was a major breakthrough for Winnie, who realised that she no longer had to hide her past to feel worthy of love and connection. She could be her true self, imperfections and all, and still be deserving.

This journey isn't always easy, and it's not a linear path. Some days will feel harder than others, but with each step, we lighten the load of shame. We begin to embrace ourselves with compassion and to trust that we are worthy of all the good things life has to offer.

As we release the burden of shame, we open ourselves to a life of freedom—freedom from self-doubt, from fear of judgement, and from the belief that we are unworthy. We discover that we are enough, not because of what we've achieved, but because of who we are at our core. And in that realisation, we find the strength to stand tall, to live authentically, and to fully embrace the beauty of our imperfect, human selves.

Practice: Unburdening Shame with Compassion

Sit or lie down comfortably in a quiet place. Close your eyes if it feels safe, or lower your gaze. Take a few slow, deep breaths, noticing the rhythm of your body. Allow your muscles to soften with each exhale.

Gently notice any thoughts, feelings, or sensations. Where does shame live in your body? Perhaps it's a tightness, a heaviness, or a whisper in your mind.

Focus on this area with curiosity and care. Notice its shape, colour, temperature, or movement. Simply be present with it.

Tune into how you feel toward this part. Can you offer it kindness, curiosity, and care? Resistance is okay, just notice it.

Ask this part what it wants you to know. What would it say if it could speak? How old does it feel? Acknowledge that it has carried this burden to protect you.

Gently reassure it that it doesn't have to hold this alone. Ask what it fears might happen if it lets go, and what it believes it is protecting. Let answers come naturally.

Visualise standing with this part, witnessing its story with compassion while remaining grounded in your breath. Invite it to release what it no longer needs. You might see it:

- *Lifted by the wind into the sky*

- *Offered to the earth to become something new*

- *Carried by water into cleansing currents*

- *Transformed by fire into light and warmth*

Allow the vision to unfold naturally, sensing the burden lifting and space opening for something new.

Take a few breaths and notice any lightness, deeper breathing, or inner knowing. Perhaps the 8 C Qualities appear - Calmness, Curiosity, Clarity, Compassion, Confidence, Creativity, Courage, Connectedness.

Thank this part for its journey and yourself for showing up. Remember you can return anytime with kindness and presence.

Gently bring awareness back to your body. Wiggle your fingers and toes. Take one deep breath, feeling the ground beneath you. Open your eyes, carrying a renewed sense of self.

You are whole. You are worthy. You are free.

Rewriting My Story

When puberty hit, my body began to change, as it does for many teenagers. I suddenly had hips, thighs, and a stomach, and I didn't know how to reconcile these changes with the image I had of myself. As a dancer, my body had always been a source of pride, a tool for expression, a thing of beauty. But with the arrival of new curves and weight, I began to feel disconnected from it. The body that once moved with grace now felt like a stranger. I looked at the slender, tall dancers around me and couldn't help but feel like I didn't belong. The comparison started early, and it stayed with me. I felt as though my body was never good enough. Not in the way society told me it should be.

This story, the one I told myself, didn't just remain a thread through my teen years. It carried me through my twenties, into motherhood, and beyond. No matter how much I achieved, no matter how I cared for my children or worked tirelessly in my career, there was always that quiet voice in my mind telling me my body didn't measure up. The shame I felt never fully left, and it became the lens through which I saw myself.

In my thirties, I decided to try a new approach. I picked up weights and threw myself into building muscle. I wanted strength, I wanted to feel powerful. And for a time, I did. I liked the way my body looked, toned and strong, but it came with a cost. I was still living in overdrive, juggling work as a police officer, raising children, and trying to keep everything else together. Movement was no longer about joy. It was about pushing my body to meet expectations, to prove its worth. I didn't realise it then, but my nervous system was stuck in survival mode, constantly running on stress and adrenaline. I kept pushing, even when my body whispered that it had had enough.

But eventually, my body couldn't keep up. It said no. It shut down. The body that I had worked so hard to transform, that I had pushed to its limits, entered a state of freeze. I became numb. My nervous system, constantly stuck in fight or flight, collapsed into a space where everything felt distant, disconnected, and out of reach. This was my body's way of saying, "Enough."

In this state, I gained twenty kilos. It wasn't just physical weight, it was emotional weight too. My body was holding onto years of stress, of survival, of unheeded signals. It was trying to protect me in the only way it knew how. The weight wasn't about food, exercise, or lack thereof, it was my body's response to the decades of pressure, expectations, and unresolved trauma.

This marked a turning point in my journey. It was time to rewrite my story. I realised that I had been living with a belief that my body was something to control, something to hide, something to be ashamed of. But what if my body wasn't something to be feared or controlled? What if it was a source of wisdom, of guidance, of strength? What if I could release the shame and step into a new narrative?

To release the burden of shame, we must also rewrite the narrative we've been carrying. Instead of seeing ourselves as broken or unworthy, we can choose to see ourselves as resilient, capable, and deserving of love and success.

Rewriting my story meant learning to let go of the beliefs I had held for so long. It meant releasing the idea that my worth was tied to how my body looked, how it performed, or how it conformed to societal ideals. It meant embracing the fullness of my body, not as something to be ashamed of, but as something to be honoured. I began to listen to my body with love and patience, to honour its needs instead of overriding them. I had to learn to rest without guilt, to move with compassion, to stop punishing myself for not fitting a mould.

In the years since, I've been gently, somatically reconnecting with my body. It hasn't been quick. It's been a slow and sacred process, but it's been necessary. I've had to unlearn decades of conditioning that told me my worth was tied to the way I looked or how much I could push myself. Instead, I'm learning to honour my body's rhythms and its wisdom. I'm slowly thawing the freeze, releasing the layers of armour I once wore to protect myself.

Rewriting my story is not just about the physical transformation, it's about emotional and mental liberation. It's about recognising that my body, in all its imperfections, is a source of beauty and power. It is not something to be ashamed of. It is something to be celebrated. I am learning to embrace every part of me, from the stretch marks to the scars, from the soft curves to the strong muscles. They tell my story, a story of survival, resilience, and now, healing.

This journey is ongoing, but with each step, I am reclaiming my body as my own. I am learning to listen to it, trust it, and love it. The shame that once weighed me down no longer holds power over me. I am rewriting my story, and in doing so, I am finding freedom, strength, and compassion.

Embodied Insight
What would it feel like to rewrite your own story?
What if you could release the shame and embrace your body with
love and acceptance, just as it is? What would it look like to honour
your body's wisdom and rhythms?

When I Dropped to My Knees

As a mother of four, life is a whirlwind of motion. Messy, beautiful, and undeniably chaotic. Ashton's diagnosis of neurodivergence marked the beginning of a chapter I never expected but was deeply meant to walk.

From the very beginning, embracing Ashton's neurodivergence felt natural. It was never something to fix but something to honour. His mind, his nervous system, his way of experiencing the world were uniquely his. With this acceptance came a path of learning, filled with speech therapists, occupational therapists, behavioural support. While I was grateful for the help, trying to balance the needs of all my children while coordinating Ashton's therapies stretched me beyond measure.

When the twins started kindergarten, the challenges Ashton faced became more visible. The early excitement of school gave way to difficulty adjusting to the expectations of the classroom. The structured routine, new faces, and sensory demands of the classroom became too much for him. He would hide under tables, growl like a lion, throw chairs, and have big meltdowns. Nearly every day, the school would call. Sometimes concerned. Sometimes, it felt like they were judging. I was always advocating. Always explaining. Always trying to help others see my son for who he truly was.

At home, the emotional toll was immense. I was exhausted. Trying to support Ashton, care for my other children, and hold the family together took everything I had. I found myself snapping more often than I wanted to. Raising my voice. Feeling frustrated. But beneath all of that was something even heavier. Shame.

Shame whispered that I was failing. That I wasn't doing enough. That I wasn't enough. It crept into the quiet moments and clung to the loud ones. I questioned everything. Why can't I make this easier for him? Why am I not more patient? Why does this feel so hard?

Then one day, after another call from the school and another early pickup, I broke. After the children were asleep, I collapsed onto my bed and cried. A flood of tears I could no longer hold in. I wept into the pillows. Kicked the blankets. Let it all pour out.

Eventually, I dropped to my knees. My hands on the ground. My body heavy with the weight of everything I had been carrying. In that rawness, something old and familiar rose up from within. Inspired by the traditional Hawaiian practice of Ho'oponopono[17], a sacred process of reconciliation and forgiveness, I placed my hands over my heart and began to speak the words, offering them to myself.

I'm sorry
Please forgive me
Thank you
I love you

I shared these words to myself because I was ready to offer myself something I hadn't in a long time: compassion, forgiveness, grace, and love.

I'm sorry for expecting myself to do this perfectly
Please forgive me for the ways I have judged myself
Thank you for staying, for trying, for loving through it all
I love you for everything you are and everything you're still becoming

With every repetition, shame began to loosen. I saw clearly how I had taken on the burden of trying to control everything. How I had pushed myself and Ashton toward an unreachable standard, hoping to protect him from misunderstanding and protect myself from being seen as a bad mother. But it was never about being perfect. It was always about being present.

That night something inside me softened. I let go of the weight of others' opinions and re-centred myself around what really mattered. My priority became clear. Not to prove anything. But to support Ashton. And to support myself.

I could not be there for him if I was constantly abandoning myself. I began to shift. I stopped trying to fix. I started listening. I reminded Ashton that it was okay to struggle. That he was loved no matter what. And as I did, I started speaking to myself in the same way.

I noticed I was snapping less. I was breathing more. I began to notice the build-up before the overwhelm and reach for my tools—grounding, support, co-regulation. I began to mother myself with the same grace I offered my children.

The Ho'oponopono prayer became a rhythm I returned to often, quietly in the car, whispered under my breath, or through tears. This practice helped lift the dimensions of shame that had settled in my body. It reminded me I didn't need to be perfect to be loving. That I didn't need to hold it all together to be whole. I could keep learning, keep softening, and keep returning.

Motherhood hasn't become easier, but it has become more sacred. I no longer measure my worth by how together I appear or how well I manage it all. I measure it by how gently I return, to love, to presence, to grace.

In embracing the mess and forgiving the missteps, I found something even more powerful than control. I found connection. I found truth. I found myself.

Embodied Insight
*Where in your life are you holding yourself to impossible standards,
and what might soften if you whispered "I'm sorry, please forgive me,
thank you, I love you" to yourself there?*

# Good Girl Reimagined

I was always the good girl. The one who did her homework on time, raised her hand in class, and followed the rules without question. As a child, I prided myself on being responsible, on knowing what was expected of me and delivering it flawlessly. I was praised for my maturity, for my ability to anticipate the needs of others before they were spoken. My gold stars lined up neatly, reaffirming my worthiness.

As I grew older, being the good girl extended beyond the classroom. I became the reliable one, the one who kept things together when others couldn't. I listened when people needed to vent, stayed quiet when my opinions didn't align, and made choices that kept me in the realm of acceptability. I worked hard, did what I was supposed to do, and walked the path of achievement. From the outside, it looked like success.

But inside, it felt like a cage.

At some point, I started resenting the good girl. I saw how she kept me small, how she stopped me from speaking up when something felt wrong, how she prioritised approval over authenticity. And I hated her for it.

I felt ashamed of her willingness to please, to mould herself into what others wanted. I started to believe that being good meant being weak, that it made me easy to manipulate, too soft, too naïve. The world rewarded me for my goodness, but inside, I felt like a fraud, like I had built an identity that wasn't truly mine.

So I tried to silence her. I thought that if I could push her away, I could finally feel free.

In my attempt to escape the good girl, I swung in the opposite direction. I chased rebellion, believing it was the antidote to the perfectionism that had imprisoned me. As a teenager, I sought escape in alcohol, recklessness, and a rejection of anything that felt like discipline or responsibility. I convinced myself that I was finally living on my terms.

But I wasn't free. I was just lost.

What I thought was rebellion was actually self-destruction. I wasn't making choices from a place of empowerment. I was reacting from a place of pain. My rebellion wasn't about reclaiming myself, it was about punishing the good girl inside me. I blamed her for my years of restriction, for the exhaustion of always trying to be enough. And so I sabotaged myself, thinking that if I could just destroy everything she had built, I would finally feel whole.

I didn't realise that I had simply moved from one shadow to another—the shadow of the good girl to the shadow of the rebel, where chaos and self-sabotage ruled just as strongly as control and perfection had before.

Even when I thought I had outgrown the good girl, she still had her hold on me. When I became a detective, I knew I was capable. I was great at my job. But when it came to my superiors, I was still that little girl in school, worried I had done something wrong. I took on every case I could, desperate to prove myself, eager to please, unable to say no.

I recall moments when I felt stretched beyond my limits, yet I still said "yes" to every request, every additional task. *Because that's what a good girl does, right?* She is reliable. She is responsible. She doesn't push back. Even when exhaustion settled into my bones, even when resentment started to creep in, I kept going. Because I had been conditioned to believe that saying "no" was selfish. That rest was indulgent. That my worth was tied to how much I could give.

Until I couldn't give anymore.

Burnout wasn't just exhaustion, it was a reckoning. My body shut down before my mind was ready to accept the truth. I couldn't keep living like this. I had spent years running on adrenaline, living in a constant state of fight, flight, or freeze. The awareness of my conditioning finally caught up with me.

I had a choice: continue down the path of depletion, or finally, finally listen to the voice within me that had been whispering all along.

Healing meant unlearning. It meant stepping away from the version of 'good' that had been conditioned into me, the one that told me my worth depended on my ability to please. Instead of self-suppression, I embraced self-expression. Instead of perfectionism, I chose authenticity.

I took time to nurture my nervous system, to step away from the constant activation and into safety. I allowed myself to rest, breathe, and listen. It was in this stillness my intuition spoke.

It told me to establish boundaries.
It told me my service did not define my worth to others.
It told me that I could be the good girl. Not in her shadow form, but in her light form.

The reimagined good girl knows that "no" is a complete sentence. She recognises that rest is not weakness, it is necessary for longevity and impact. She leads with self-respect, not martyrdom.

I stepped forth to those around me, to my colleagues and superiors, and I established my boundaries. I no longer operated from a place of fear. I no longer needed to prove my worth.

Instead of shrinking, I expanded.
Instead of silencing myself, I spoke up.
Instead of abandoning myself, I prioritised me.

The good girl, in her highest form, is sovereign. She honours her truth. She is radiant, intuitive, and free. And she no longer needs permission to take up space.

She is radiant, self-trusting, and whole.
She is me. I am her. I am whole.

In learning to accept her, I l earnt to accept myself. I don't have to choose between being 'good' or being 'free.' I can be both. I can be good in a way that is expansive, that honours my truth, that allows me to live with both strength and softness.

The good girl was never meant to be abandoned.
She was meant to be reimagined.
And now, I let her shine.

Embodied Insight
*Reflect on the 'good girl' within you. What are the ways you have
been conditioned to please or perform for approval? How has this
affected your sense of self and your actions?
How can you reimagine the 'good girl', bringing those qualities into
balance with your authentic voice and power?*

Loyalty to Fear

We are so loyal to our fear. It is almost second nature to us now. We can be in the middle of a beautiful moment, laughing with a loved one, soaking in the sun, or feeling a sudden rush of peace, and in a split second, fear slides in like a shadow. Thoughts like "This will not last," or "Do not get too comfortable," or "Something bad is going to happen," sneak in quietly and steal the moment.

Without even realising it, we drop our joy. Not because we want to, but because we have been trained to. Conditioned to believe that joy is temporary, fragile, even dangerous. We have been taught to be loyal to our fear, to see it as responsible, smart, protective. And so we follow it. We let it lead, even when it leads us away from ourselves.

This loyalty is not something we consciously chose. It was woven into us, threaded through family patterns, societal expectations, cultural norms, institutions, and generations of unspoken rules. We are born into legacies. Into belief systems. Into traditions and institutionalised ways of being. And when we begin to question them, shame often arrives.

There is the shame of no longer fitting into the mould. The shame of asking, "What if this way does not work for me?" The shame of starting to honour the quiet truth within us, even when it goes against everything we have been told to follow.

Traditions can be beautiful. They can ground us, provide community, and create connection. But when traditions are placed heavily on our shoulders, they can also become cages, especially when they demand we abandon parts of ourselves to belong.

For me, this was most apparent in motherhood. Earlier in this book, I shared how I began screening phone calls from my children's school. There was a season when those calls came often, telling me my son wasn't meeting expectations—he had done something wrong, or wasn't 'fitting in.' Each call sliced through me with shame and a heavy sense of failure. It felt like a constant reminder that I, or he, was getting it wrong.

Then there were the good days. Days when he came home full of stories, when he'd had a great day, engaged in learning, connected, and grown. I would feel joy bloom in my chest, a breath of relief and gratitude. But I wouldn't allow myself to stay in it for long. Almost instantly, fear would creep in. "What if this doesn't last?" "What if tomorrow brings another meltdown?" "What if the next phone call undoes all of this?"

That joy would slip away. Not because it wasn't real, but because fear had taught me not to trust it. That's the loyalty fear demands. It convinces us that it's safer to brace for disappointment than to risk the vulnerability of trusting things could go well. It tells us it's safer to expect the worst.

But somewhere along the way, I began to question that loyalty to fear. It wasn't an overnight revelation, but more of a subtle unravelling. I found myself in moments of stillness, perhaps late at night, after another difficult conversation with the school, or in the quiet after a particularly hard day, and I began to ask myself, *Why am I holding onto this fear?* Why was I following a script that said I had to be perfect, composed, and in control at all times? I realised that the traditions I had clung to, those of being a flawless mother, of measuring my success by external expectations, didn't fit anymore. They were suffocating, forcing me into a mould that wasn't mine.

It was in those moments of questioning that I started to listen to the quiet part of me, my Intuitive Intelligence®, the one that had always been there but had been overshadowed by fear and expectation. That quiet voice reminded me that my son wasn't broken, that I wasn't broken, and that perhaps it wasn't us who needed fixing. Maybe the real change needed to happen within the system, the structures that had failed to see and support our uniqueness. The moment I allowed myself to hear that quiet truth was the first step toward releasing the grip of fear and embracing a new way forward.

That shift didn't happen immediately. It came gently, piece by piece. It happened through supporting my nervous system, creating safety within my body and my life. It happened through expanding my capacity for love and trust. It came from releasing the fear that had kept me tightly bound. And it came through learning to follow my intuition, even when it defied logic.

This journey was not about choosing one truth over another. It was about choosing truth over fear. And in that choice, I began to release the shame fear had woven into every part of me.

To do that, I had to break up with fear. Not in one big dramatic moment, but in quiet, consistent ways. By saying yes to my inner knowing. Yes to the beauty in moments, even when they felt fleeting. Yes to being fully me, and fully my son's mother, even when that did not fit the traditional expectation.

Unpacking our loyalty to fear is sacred work. It is the moment we stop betraying ourselves to make others comfortable. It is the moment we realise that shame does not belong to us. It was handed to us. And we do not have to carry it anymore.

So if you are reading this and feeling like you have been hiding parts of yourself to belong, if joy feels fleeting, or authenticity feels risky, please remember you are not alone. Your inner truth is not a betrayal. You are allowed to expand beyond what others understand.

Release the inherited shame. Choose presence over fear. And remember, joy is not a trap. It is your compass home.

Graceful Reminder

You are not here to be loyal to your fear. You are here to be loyal to your becoming.

The Graceful Shedding

THERE COMES A MOMENT IN EVERY HEALING JOURNEY WHEN YOU GROW
TIRED OF CARRYING WHAT WAS NEVER YOURS TO HOLD.
SHAME IS HEAVY. STICKY. QUIET. SUBTLE. LOUD.
IT NESTLES IN YOUR CHEST, DISGUISING ITSELF AS GUILT,
UNWORTHINESS, OR NOT-ENOUGHNESS.
AND FOR A LONG TIME, YOU MIGHT BELIEVE IT'S JUST A PART OF YOU.
BUT MAYBE, JUST MAYBE, IT WAS NEVER YOURS TO BEGIN WITH.
MAYBE SHAME WAS SOMETHING YOU LEARNT TO CARRY TO STAY SAFE.
SOMETHING ABSORBED, NOT BORN WITHIN YOU.
SOMETHING INHERITED, NOT CHOSEN.

YOU DIDN'T FAIL. YOU ADAPTED.
YOU DIDN'T BREAK. YOU PROTECTED YOURSELF.

AND NOW, YOU GET TO CHOOSE SOMETHING DIFFERENT.

YOU ARE ALLOWED TO SAY,
"I NO LONGER CARRY SHAME FOR THE WAY MY BODY RESPONDED TO
TRAUMA."
"I NO LONGER CARRY SHAME FOR NEEDING TIME, REST, SPACE, AND
SOFTNESS."
"I NO LONGER CARRY SHAME FOR THE WAYS I'VE PROTECTED MYSELF."
"I NO LONGER CARRY SHAME FOR THE TRUTH OF WHO I AM."
THIS IS NOT ABOUT REJECTING THE PAST. THIS IS ABOUT RELEASING
THE BURDEN IT PLACED UPON YOUR SHOULDERS.

EMBODIED GRACE

You are not broken. You never were.
You are becoming.
And becoming requires shedding.

So let yourself unravel.
Let the shame melt away like old skin no longer needed.
Let your heart breathe without the weight.
Let grace hold the parts that still feel tender.

You are safe.
You are loved.
You are free to rise.
Unburdened, unashamed, and whole.

PART EIGHT

Radical Acceptance

Wholeness of You

I remember sitting across from Tanja as she held her breath, trying to swallow the weight of her pain. Tears brimmed, not because she wanted to cry, but because she had spent a lifetime resisting the urge.

"I should not feel this way. I should be over it by now," she whispered.

These were not just passing thoughts. They were judgements. Walls she had built over the years to guard herself from discomfort. But walls do not just keep pain out. They keep us in.

I knew this all too well. As a detective, I learnt how to tuck emotions away, to separate pain from function, and to keep going. Vulnerability was not an option. There was no room to pause. No space to feel. Only through my somatic healing did I learn the truth. We cannot move forward without first meeting ourselves fully and gently, right where we are.

This is the beginning of radical acceptance.

Radical acceptance is not about giving in or pretending everything is fine. It is about turning toward what is true without flinching. It means meeting pain, fear, or shame with the quiet courage to say, "I see you. You are allowed to be here." As Tara Brach teaches, healing begins when we welcome our experience with compassion rather than resistance.

To embody grace is to remember that your worth is not something you have to earn. It is not dependent on how well you perform or how perfectly you appear. Worthiness is already within you. When we soften the grip of perfection and begin to see our beauty even in the places we once disowned, something sacred unfolds. A deeper connection to self.

For many, this journey begins with discomfort. We fear that accepting ourselves as we are might invite rejection, either from others or from within. And so we stay in self-criticism, hiding parts of ourselves in shame. But true self-compassion arises when we bring those hidden parts into the light. When we choose to accept the whole of who we are. In doing so, we create an inner refuge. A space safe enough to explore, to heal, and to grow.

Our bodies remember what our minds often try to forget. They carry the stories, the sorrow, the survival. Trauma research, like that of Bessel van der Kolk, affirms this. Healing requires a return to the body. This is why radical acceptance must be embodied.

Tanja had long been disconnected from her body. The grief that lived in her chest had been pushed aside for years. When I gently invited her to place a hand on her heart and breathe, she hesitated.

"It feels like if I let go, I will fall apart," she said.

I nodded. "What if falling apart is the beginning of coming back together?"

She exhaled. I saw the softening. The tender surrender to what is. This is the essence of radical acceptance. Creating the internal conditions for self-compassion to grow. Not through force, but through presence.

When we stop fighting our experience, change begins to move through us. When we stop rejecting parts of ourselves, healing finds a way in. We do not have to like what arises. We simply need to make room for it.

One of the greatest misunderstandings is the idea that acceptance means settling. But it is the opposite. Acceptance does not keep us stuck. It sets us free. It allows us to meet life as it is and choose how we move with it, rather than against it.

To lean into discomfort is to face what lies beneath the surface, the tender parts we rarely let others see or even acknowledge in ourselves. Transformation begins in these vulnerable places, where we allow ourselves to be fully present with what is.

Wholeness is not perfection. It is the courageous act of embracing all that you are. The known and the mysterious. The soft and the strong. The broken and the becoming. True integration happens not when we fix ourselves, but when we finally stop separating and begin welcoming every part of our being.

Radical acceptance calls you back to yourself. As you meet each part of you with compassion, the fear of judgement fades, and in its place rises a quiet belonging. And this belonging, rooted in grace, does not just heal you. It touches everyone you meet.

This is the grace of acceptance.
This is the expansion of trust.
This is the beginning of coming home.

Embodied Insight

What part of you have you been resisting, and what might begin to shift if you met it with compassion instead of judgment?

Trusting What Is

Long before I stopped drinking, my Intuitive Intelligence® was guiding me. It did not shout. It spoke with an assertive knowing that alcohol no longer served me. But my ego resisted. It told me I was fine, that I deserved to relax, that I could handle it. I listened for a long time because change felt threatening, like losing part of who I was.

Eventually, I chose to trust the voice of certainty. It was a slow and layered journey, more about healing my nervous system than just quitting a habit. Alcohol had numbed my feelings for years. Without it, I had to learn to be present with discomfort, to feel rather than avoid. This was where I met challenges and resistance within. I replaced alcohol with sugar. Chocolate and biscuits became my new comfort. Beneath that was the same old belief. I was not good enough, not worthy of love without conditions.

I gained twenty kilograms and avoided mirrors. But one day, trying on a favourite pair of pants that no longer fit, the shame hit me hard. The inner critic was loud. Right then, I paused. Instead of spiralling into self-judgement, I placed my hand on my heart and said, "I embrace my journey with love and understanding."

This simple practice became my daily ritual. Standing in front of the mirror, touching a part of my body and looking directly into my eyes, I repeated those words, softly and firmly. It was a way of meeting myself with kindness and truth, creating safety within my body for the shame and discomfort to be held and gently released.

Radical acceptance is not about giving up or settling. It is about acknowledging what is real without needing to fix or escape. It means saying, "This is where I am, and I can love myself, anyway." From that place, real transformation begins. I stopped resisting my body and my journey. I stopped making my worth conditional on size, control, or achievement.

Over time, I noticed I wasn't turning to food in the same way. Not because I forced myself to change, but because I no longer needed comfort to soften what I was avoiding. I was learning to meet myself with presence instead of escape. The more I practiced radical acceptance, the more my choices came from love, care, and respect for myself, and not from trying to fix or numb anything.

Radical acceptance allowed my nervous system to trust it was safe to rest, to release, and to heal. It became the foundation for growth, not perfection. My path to sobriety revealed that trust is something we embody, and it does not always feel comfortable. It is the steady choice to stay present with myself, especially in moments that feel messy or unlovable.

The true gift of radical acceptance is not arriving somewhere new but holding yourself with compassionate kindness as you walk the path of healing.

Practice: Mirror Moment

Stand comfortably in front of a mirror in good light so you can see your reflection clearly.

Feel the weight of your feet on the floor. Take a few deep breaths, inhaling through your nose and exhaling slowly through your mouth.

Look at your reflection. Notice yourself as a whole. Simply observe how you feel in this moment without labelling or judging.

Notice any parts of yourself that feel difficult or uncomfortable. See them as part of your unique journey rather than flaws.

Place one hand gently on your heart or a part of the body that calls for it. Breathe into the warmth and presence of your hand.

Send kindness and understanding to all parts of yourself, especially the parts that feel vulnerable or difficult. You might silently say words of care, or simply hold a feeling of gentle acceptance.

Spend a few moments noticing any sensations or emotions that arise. You might offer yourself words of encouragement, gratitude, or love, or simply feel a sense of warmth and acceptance.

When you feel ready, take a few more deep breaths and step back from the mirror. Carry this sense of acceptance and compassion into the rest of your day.

Homecoming

There was a time when I believed friendship meant always showing up. No matter what. That if I gave enough time, energy, and care, I would be valued in return. But I learnt that pouring endlessly into a cup that never refilled my own would leave me empty. In the beginning, I had a friend who I thought was genuine. We met through mutual connections, and at first, our conversations felt easy. But over time, a pattern emerged I was too afraid to acknowledge.

She only reached out when she needed something. Advice. A favour. A listening ear. And I answered every time, eager to be of service. Hoping that if I gave enough, a deeper bond would form. But in the spaces between her needs, my calls and messages often went unanswered. When I needed support or reached out just to connect, I was met with short replies. Our conversations ended as soon as the focus shifted away from her. Still, I tried. I kept trying because I was terrified of what it would mean if I stopped. Would it prove the belief I had carried for so long—that I was not good enough to be anyone's friend? That the only way to belong was to be needed?

Then came her separation and eventual divorce. She was heartbroken, and I truly wanted to be there for her. Whenever she called, I picked up. Whenever she needed to talk, I listened. Whenever she cried, I held space. I told myself, this is what friendship is.

But after the divorce, things changed. She met new friends. Our plans were cancelled more often, with reasons I tried to understand, only to later learn she had gone out with others instead. Still, when she needed something, she called. And still, I showed up.

Until something within me began to shift.

I wanted the friendship to survive, but I had taken on the role of fixer. I carried responsibility that was never mine to hold. The weight of her emotions and expectations became too much. I noticed how drained I felt after every call. It was not a friendship based on mutual care. It was her world, and I had become an orbit around it.

One evening, after another cancelled plan followed by the same pattern, I felt something inside me break open. The air was still, but inside, I was restless. My body was tight. My heart felt heavy. I placed a hand on my chest and took a slow, steady breath.

A question surfaced from deep within me. Do I want to keep showing up like this?

The answer did not come from my mind. It came from my body. A grounded, unwavering no. It was not angry. It was not dramatic. It was simply true. My shoulders softened. I exhaled. And I could finally see. I had been giving from fear. Fear of being rejected. Fear of not being enough. But true friendship is not something to be earned through sacrifice. It is grounded in mutual love, care, and effort. My intuition was gently guiding me to something I had long resisted. Boundaries.

This *no* came with an unexpected gift. A subtle *yes*. A *yes* that felt expansive, warm, and rooted in self-respect. A *yes* that settled deep in my body like a truth I had always known but only now allowed myself to feel.

The next time she called, I paused. I centred myself. I responded not from obligation, but from choice. I still listened, but I honoured my energy. I no longer overextended. When it felt like too much, I stepped away with care.

She noticed. She asked why I was not always available. I had a choice. To slip back into old patterns or to stand in my truth.

I chose truth.

I told her, with kindness, that I valued our friendship but needed balance.

Her response was revealing. There was no curiosity about my experience. No interest in how I felt. Just silence and withdrawal.

Once, that would have devastated me. I would have replayed every conversation, wondering what I had done wrong. But now, I could see it clearly. This was not about my worth. It was simply a reflection of where she was.

I chose to forgive her. And I chose to forgive myself. Not to excuse what happened, but to let go of the burden I had been carrying. I forgave her for what she could not give, and I forgave myself for trying to earn something that should have always been given freely.

I had entered that friendship longing for connection so deeply that I lost myself in it. I shaped myself into the version of a friend I thought she needed. Always available. Always giving. Always proving.

But true friendship is not about performance. It is not about self-sacrifice. It is about being seen, valued, and accepted as you are.

As I let go, I could feel it clearly. I had never truly been myself in that friendship. But I am now. I am no longer willing to shrink or bend myself to feel worthy. My worth was never up for negotiation. It was always within me. I was not just letting go, I was returning to myself. Over time, our contact faded. And instead of questioning what went wrong, I felt a quiet sense of peace.

Because for the first time, I had chosen me. I had asked myself a question that mattered and I had listened.

And that was the beginning of something new. Something rooted. Something balanced. Something whole. Not just for others, but for myself too.

Embodied Insight

*Think of a time when you prioritised someone else's needs over your
own in a relationship; whether a friendship, family connection, or
partnership.*
What were you afraid would happen if you didn't?
*Looking back, how did that experience shape your understanding of
your own worth?*

The Courage to Seek Support

I have experienced moments where exhaustion wrapped itself around me so tightly that I longed for an escape. I wished, not for something tragic, but for an accident just severe enough that I would be forced to rest. A situation where no one else would be harmed, something orchestrated by nature itself, a car sliding off a slick road, or a tree branch falling at just the right moment. Something that would allow me to step away from the relentless demands of life, of work, of responsibility, without feeling like I had failed.

At the time, these thoughts felt strangely logical. I never wanted to die. I simply wanted a reason, one deemed acceptable by the world, to press pause.

But when those thoughts resurfaced after I became a mother, they terrified me. The idea of my children suffering because of my absence shook me to my core. With undeniable clarity, I realised that I couldn't ignore my thoughts any longer. I needed help.

And yet, I resisted.

I had a long list of reasons why I couldn't seek support. It would cost money I'd rather spend elsewhere. I didn't have the time to sit and talk to someone. And if I'm honest, I didn't *want* to talk. The psychological sessions provided by police as a result of traumatic scenes I had attended left me feeling raw and misunderstood. They were sterile and clinical, and I didn't feel they listened to me and saw *me* as a whole person.

But the deeper truth was that I was afraid.

In my world back then as a frontline detective, seeking support for emotional struggles wasn't something I talked about. It wasn't something I did.

Vulnerability could mean restriction. If I admitted I was struggling, would it cost me my career? Would I no longer be considered capable? Who was I if I wasn't the one holding it all together?

As I delved into my studies of somatics and the nervous system, that fear shifted. I started to see support through a different lens. Not as something external that someone else had to give me, but as something I could allow myself to receive. As Carl Jung wisely said, "We cannot change anything unless we accept it." I realised that by accepting where I was, I could seek help in a way that resonated with me and felt safe.

That's when I got support from a somatic practitioner.

It changed my life.

Through working with a somatic practitioner, I discovered that healing wasn't just about talking, it was about *feeling*. I learnt that my body held the unspoken stories of my past, the stress, the trauma, the exhaustion. And as I tuned into those sensations, as I gently unravelled the tension I had carried for years, something remarkable happened.

I felt lighter. I felt more present. My physical body softened. My mind quietened. My heart opened. I no longer needed an external event to force me into rest. I was learning how to give myself permission to pause, to breathe, to *be*.

Most of all, I had to face my humility. To recognise that I am human. And that means I am not meant to do it all alone. None of us are.

Having a support team is one of the most powerful things we can create for ourselves. And the beautiful thing is, it can look different for everyone. Support doesn't just come in the form of professionals like psychologists, somatic therapists, or counsellors. It can be woven through friendships, family, mentors, or even spiritual directors. Sometimes, support is found in community spaces, online groups, or through practices like yoga, meditation, or creative expression.

There is no one-size-fits-all approach to receiving support. Some people may find solace in breathwork or energy healing, while others may need structured therapy or group coaching. What matters is that you create a network that truly nurtures you. One that meets you where you are and supports you in the ways you need most.

So I ask you, where are you resisting support because you are afraid?

What part of your ego is keeping you attached to old stories and beliefs that no longer serve you? The ones that whisper, *You should be able to handle this on your own. You don't need anyone.*

What if, instead of fearing support, you saw it as a gift? A strength rather than a mark of weakness.

And most importantly, what support team is your soul craving for you to create?

Take a moment. Breathe. Feel into your body. And listen.

Because sometimes, the bravest thing we can do is simply allow ourselves to be held.

Embodied Insight
*In what areas of your life are you hesitant to seek support, and what
fears might be holding you back?*

Always Worthy of Grace

There's a familiar story that surfaces when I feel like I've fallen short, a persistent narrative that tells me I need to be 'better' to be worthy of love. It's a story shaped by past experiences, echoed by old expectations. And it's not just mine. It's one many of us carry. Yet over time, I've come to understand something deeper: you are worthy of grace. Not because of what you do, how well you perform, or how much you give but simply because you are.

I want to share a moment that helped me truly understand this. It was an afternoon where I felt overwhelmed. I had recently started my business as an Intuitive Somatic Mentor, pouring my heart and soul into something I deeply believed in. But despite all my effort, the reality was clear. I wasn't earning an income.

I remember sitting at my desk, staring at the numbers in my bank account, feeling the panic rise in my chest. How was I going to make this work? Self-doubt crept in, whispering that maybe I wasn't cut out for this, that my dream was naïve. Would my hard work ever lead to something sustainable?

The pressure pressed down on me, my chest tightening with every passing thought. No matter how many hours I worked or how much energy I poured in, it felt like nothing was shifting. The voice in my head grew louder. "You're failing. You're not enough."

I stepped outside to clear my head and spotted a flower growing through a crack in the pavement. Its petals were slightly torn, its leaves imperfect, but it stood there, vibrant and alive.

I paused, staring at this tiny, unexpected reminder of beauty in the messiness of life.

That flower didn't need to be flawless to be worthy of sunlight or soil. It simply existed. And that was enough. That's when I understood I didn't have to earn my place either. My worth wasn't tied to the number in my bank account or how 'perfectly' I built my business. It was inherent.

We, too, are like that flower. Grace is not something we earn through effort or accomplishment. It is something we allow ourselves to receive. It is the softening that happens when we stop trying to be 'enough' and realise that we already are.

But I get it. Believing this isn't always easy. We live in a world that measures worth by success, productivity, and perfection. We're taught to hide our flaws, to fix what's "wrong," and to hustle for our place in the world.

Yet grace whispers something entirely different. "You are loved. You are enough. You belong."

Grace doesn't wait for you to be ready. It meets you where you are—in the mess, the heartbreak, the uncertainty. It doesn't care if you've made mistakes, if you've struggled, or if you feel unworthy. Grace sees beyond all of that, straight to the truth of your being.

When you feel least deserving of grace, that's when you need it the most.

Imagine a child learning to walk. They stumble. They fall.

You wouldn't withhold love from that child. You'd scoop them up, encourage them, remind them of their goodness.

Why should it be any different now?

Grace doesn't come with conditions.

It is the truth that no matter how far you wander, or how tangled things get, you are already home in yourself.

Graceful Reminder

Grace is not given when you are perfect. It arrives when you remember you don't need to be.

Honouring Needs and Creating Boundaries

Self-acceptance is often seen as a destination, finally embracing ourselves as we are. But really, it is a journey that begins with honouring our needs and setting boundaries. These are not selfish acts but essential steps to cultivate radical self-acceptance. By listening to our inner wisdom and protecting our energy, we create space for our truest selves to thrive.

For me, this journey began when I felt overwhelmed and disconnected. Life with four kids, therapies, school, extracurricular activities, and work was full. My nervous system wasn't just stretched, it was stuck in survival mode, barely catching a breath.

In that chaos, I abandoned myself. I stopped the practices that supported my nervous system, those that grounded me. My days revolved around others' needs, leaving no space for me. Exhaustion and resentment built up and I found myself snapping at those I loved. Guilt and disconnection grew alongside.

The turning point came when I saw the cost of ignoring my needs. It depleted me and eroded my self-worth. I knew I had to change. I began to explore what honouring my needs and boundaries could look like, not just for me but for my family. It felt uncomfortable at first. I struggled with guilt, having always prioritised others. But slowly, I found my way back.

I started small, carving out moments each morning for gentle movement, breathwork, meditation, tapping or journaling. These short rituals grounded me and clarified the day ahead.

One of the biggest shifts was learning to set and maintain boundaries. For years, I let others' demands drain my energy. I realised boundaries were not about shutting people out but about protecting my energy so I could show up authentically. I became clear on what mattered and said no to what drained me. This included work and social commitments.

I also learnt to communicate my needs clearly in other areas of life. For example, I set limits around work and social obligations that felt overwhelming. I started saying no when invitations or requests didn't align with my energy or values. At home, I shared with my family how important it was for me to have daily time to recharge. Whether it was a quiet walk, journaling, or simply breathing, I held this time as non-negotiable. Setting these boundaries helped me protect my energy so I could show up fully and authentically for those I love.

Through these changes, I learnt to listen deeply to my body's signals, tension, overwhelm, unease, and ask what I needed. Sometimes rest, sometimes pause. These moments built a sense of safety within me, the foundation for radical self-acceptance.

Honouring my needs and boundaries shifted not only me but also my family and community. I felt more present and aligned, showing up with more patience and compassion. My relationships deepened and I noticed how my self-care inspired others to prioritise themselves.

Along the way, I found the power of connection. I sought out communities for support and created my own, the Connection Membership, a space where people come together to prioritise themselves, cultivate self-compassion, and honour their nervous systems.

Radical self-acceptance means choosing every day to say, "I matter." Your needs are valid, your boundaries necessary, and your wellbeing worth protecting. By listening to your inner wisdom and integrating somatic awareness, you create a life where self-acceptance is not just possible, it is inevitable.

Embodied Insight

Reflect on a time when you ignored your own needs. How did this impact your emotional, mental, or physical state? What would it have looked like to honour those needs instead?

Sacred Imprints

As we soften into the truth of who we are, we release the burden of who we were told to be. We no longer shrink ourselves to fit others expectations. Instead, we expand into the fullness of our being, unashamed and unbound.

As we meet our reflections with love, we no longer see flaws. We see stories, lived experiences, and the sacred imprints of a life deeply felt. Every scar, wrinkle, and imperfection is a reflection of our journey.

As we embrace the parts of us we once hid, we reclaim our wholeness, no matter who messy and uncomfortable the process is. Each component is necessary and worthy.

As we release the shame that was never ours to carry, we step into a new way of being. One where we no longer apologise for who we are.

As we trust that our worth is not something to be earned but something that has always been, we lay down the struggle, the striving, the self-doubt. We remember that we are inherently enough, simply because we are here.

As we offer ourselves the grace we so freely give to others, we become our own sanctuary. No longer seeking validation from the outside, we find home within.

As we walk this path of radical self-acceptance, we honour the divine within us. We choose love over judgement, compassion over criticism, and truth over fear.

And so it is, and it is so.

PART NINE

Devotion

Everyday Devotion

Connection is at the heart of devotion to God, the universe, and the life that moves through and around us. It is the attention we bring to what matters most, the way we return to love, presence, and purpose. It arises from longing, from the impulse to stay close to what sustains us, and to bring care into the world. It is the conscious choice to show up fully, lovingly, and intentionally.

True commitment to the sacred is not earned through discipline or force. It does not live in perfect rituals or daily routines. It asks only for sincerity, the simple promise to return even when life pulls us away from our centre.

For a long time, I imagined that living with this kind of reverence required long meditations, perfectly arranged spaces, and complete silence. Yet life rarely offers that luxury. Still, I found it in small moments. Pausing before I speak, answering with care instead of reaction, feeling sunlight on my face, preparing a meal with love, giving without expectation. These everyday acts carry the same intention, and they are enough.

Presence can be found in stillness or action. Some days it is lighting a candle, journaling, or simply breathing deeply. Other days it is putting the phone aside to show up fully in a conversation, helping someone, or taking necessary action even when inconvenient. Sometimes it is crying when sadness rises, letting held-back tears flow freely. Other times it is expressing anger, setting boundaries, or standing firm in what feels true. All of it is a practice of returning to what matters.

Most mornings, I step into the shower, the warm water washing over me. The night may have been restless, the children waking, my thoughts spinning, and the day ahead looming large. I place my hand on chest, close my eyes, and I offer the morning, the day, and myself to God, to the universe, to the life that moves through and around me. I ask only to be guided, to see what needs my attention with love and clarity. As the water traces down my body, each droplet feels like a reminder of presence, surrender, and devotion. This connection flows into every choice, every gesture, and every breath of the day. Even in the ordinary rhythm of life, devotion is alive.

This way of being flows through every action, choice, and breath. It does not need to be witnessed or validated by anyone else, but it is always felt deeply by ourselves. The most profound gestures often go unseen. Saying no when our body speaks, choosing rest, forgiving ourselves, helping quietly, acting from love rather than obligation. Not because we earned it, but because our hearts guide us there.

To live in this way is to stay in relationship with ourselves, with grace, with the world, and with God. It does not ask for perfection. It asks for presence, courage, and the willingness to show up even when we feel tired, uncertain, or undeserving. In that showing up, trust grows, compassion deepens, and love flows. This is not about doing more, but about being fully present, fully engaged, and fully alive in every moment.

Embodied Insight
*Where in your life are you being invited to return, not out of duty,
but out of love?*

Dancing Alone, Dancing Free

As a child, I have vivid memories of dancing, movement that wasn't choreographed by anyone else but was intuitively guided by my body. The swirling, the swaying, the smiles, the laughter, and the tears, it was a pure and raw expression of what I was feeling in the moment. Sometimes there was music accompanying me, and other times, the music flowed from within. It was my way of translating emotions into motion, a silent language allowing me to connect deeply with my inner world.

As I transitioned into young adulthood, my Thursdays, Fridays, and Saturdays were often spent in clubs, dancing until the early hours of the morning. In those moments, it felt as though society was giving me permission to continue being playful, moving in the way my body naturally desired, an extension of the freedom I had experienced as a child. The rhythm of the night seemed to honour and mirror the freedom I found within myself.

However, in my thirties, there came a shift. The carefree dances of the past faded, and dancing late into the night in high heels became a distant memory. Somewhere along the way, I forgot that movement is more than just an external expression. It is a profound way to cultivate safety within my nervous system, to connect with myself, and to support my healing. I had lost the simple joy of giving myself permission to play, move, to feel, and to be. It took time to remember that grace can be found both in playfulness and devotion, and that it is through movement that we can truly reconnect with ourselves and the rhythms of our body.

It wasn't until I had children, as I held them and watched them learn to crawl, stand, and move, that the permission I had given myself to dance returned. I would dance with my baby (or babies when I had the twins) and all my children together, and that feeling of embracing freedom and release of emotion returned. On movie nights at home, when the credits began to roll, the tradition in our house is for all of us to stand and dance away. To have fun, to play, to move and we'd be in stitches of laughter together.

One night, after I had tucked the kids into bed and kissed them goodnight, I journalled about how much I loved dancing after movie night. Then, an intuitive whisper within me asked, "What is stopping you from dancing when the kids aren't with you?" I paused, and as the question settled in, I realised something profound. The freedom I had once felt, moving my body without limitations, had somehow faded over time. In the hustle of adult life, with its expectations, responsibilities, and the subtle pressures of 'grown-up' living, I had unintentionally closed off that part of myself. I had forgotten that dancing wasn't just a way to entertain myself, it was a way to reconnect with the essence of who I am, to release stored emotions, and to feel more fully alive.

The realisation hit me deeply. There was nothing stopping me from dancing when my children weren't around, except for the barriers I had unknowingly built within myself. I had given myself permission to move freely when I was with them, but I had placed restrictions on myself when I was alone. Why should the joy of dancing be limited by circumstance or time? Why couldn't I embrace this expression of freedom, joy, and release just for me?

That night, I made a commitment to reclaim that part of me, to dance simply because I could. I started with small moments, playing music when I was alone and allowing my body to move in any way it felt called to. At first, it was a little awkward, a bit forced, but slowly, the more I did it, the more I remembered how healing movement truly is. I began to feel lighter, more grounded, and more connected to my inner self. It was a reminder that grace is not just something we offer to others. It's something we can give ourselves in the simple, beautiful act of moving our bodies in joy and expression.

Dancing became a sacred space for me again, a form of self-compassion. It wasn't about perfection, and it certainly wasn't about how it looked to others. It was simply a return to a feeling of freedom. Through movement, I found a way to release tension, to honour my body's needs, and to nurture my nervous system. I started to trust that my body knew what it needed, and the more I listened, the more fluid and expansive my sense of grace became, both in playfulness and devotion.

This practice of dancing through life, whether I'm with my children, in the quiet of my home, or just in the stillness of my heart, reminds me that grace is something we can tap into at any moment. It's the gentle acceptance of where we are and the willingness to move through life with compassion for ourselves.

Practice: Soulful Movement

Find a place where your body can move freely. You might choose to be barefoot, feeling the earth beneath you.

Close your eyes, take a few deep breaths, and simply notice how your body feels in stillness. This is your foundation, the quiet that holds grace.

Play a song that brings you joy. Let your body respond naturally. Start small, perhaps a sway of the shoulders or a gentle lift of the arms. There is no need to do anything right, just follow your body.

Feel your muscles, your joints, your breath. Notice the subtle shifts and sensations as your body wakes up and flows.

Release any need to look a certain way or move perfectly. The grace is in your experience, in the pleasure of being fully present.

If your body wants to move bigger, let it. If it wants to pause or slow, honour that too. Follow your own rhythm.

As the music ends, gradually return to stillness. Stand, sit, or lie down. Place your hands on your heart and breathe deeply. Feel gratitude for your body, for the joy that has moved through you, and for the grace you have allowed.

Stars Above, Stillness Within

Small, meaningful steps remind us we are all part of a greater consciousness, interconnected in ways we cannot fully comprehend. Have you ever experienced a moment so profound that it seemed to crystallise the beauty and interconnectedness of existence? For me, it happened in India.

It was 5 a.m., and I found myself awake, curiosity stirring within me. Rather than reaching for my phone, I chose to embrace the early hours differently. I decided to go for a swim. Aliveness, I realised, is an act of devotion to the present moment, so I welcomed it without hesitation. As I walked to the pool, the cool morning air carried a sense of calm. The water in the pool was just cool enough to refresh but not so cold as to deter me. Without reluctance, I stepped in, feeling the sensation of the water as it embraced me. Each movement felt deliberate yet effortless, a reminder of how small actions—each one taken with purpose—can ground us in the here and now.

As I leaned back to float, the sky opened above me, vast and infinite, adorned with a tapestry of countless stars. Suddenly, my body felt weightless, and the enormity of the sky enveloped me in its majesty. The universe seemed unfathomable in its immensity, its mysteries stretching far beyond anything I could measure or name. Yet, within that vastness, I felt a quiet sense of belonging. My life, small in the grand scheme of things, was still undeniably significant. I recognised myself as a thread woven into the greater fabric of existence, a vital part of a picture I could not fully see but trusted to be beautiful.

As I floated, gazing upward, I noticed how the small steps that led me her—choosing curiosity, walking to the pool, stepping into the water, and surrendering to stillness—were acts of grace in themselves. Each one was an act of devotion and a surrender to what life offered. A shift occurred within me. Instead of asking, "What meaning can life offer me?" I found myself asking, "What is life asking of me?" It was a question that invited me to participate, to respond with intention and grace. Life's meaning, I realised, is not something handed to us. It is something we co-create through our choices and our devotion to living with purpose.

I began to see that meaning isn't something we find, it's something we create through the way we show up to life. It's an act of love, a conversation with the universe, where we respond to its invitations with our actions, our courage, and our grace. Each still moment invites us to listen. Each movement, no matter how small, invites us to respond. In this dance, we begin to feel not only more connected to life but more *alive* within it. Floating beneath that vast sky, I came to understand that we don't need to chase meaning. We embody it. With each breath, each choice, each gesture of presence, we become the living expression of what life is asking of us.

Embodied Insight
As you gaze at the stars, what messages is the universe sharing with you? How can you open yourself to listen more deeply?

Grains of Devotion

During my time of writing this book, Grant, the kids and I spent a few days away during the summer school holidays. We spent long, unhurried days at the beach, where time seemed to stretch and blend with the rhythms of the ocean. With the play, laughter, and the ebb and flow of the tides, I found myself mesmerised by something seemingly simple yet profoundly grounding—sand.

At first glance, sand appears unremarkable, just tiny grains beneath our feet. But as I stood there, holding a handful of it, I felt its ancient wisdom and infinite presence. Each grain has its own story, shaped by the forces of wind, water, and time, a fragment of something once whole. Sand is a reminder of transformation, of how nature continually reshapes itself, breaking down, softening, and finding new form. It is the Earth's memory in motion.

Sand invites us into stillness. Its softness cushions us, urging us to pause and sink into the present moment. And yet, its impermanence whispers to us about the ever-changing nature of life. How even the smallest actions, over time, shape who we are. In the way sand holds imprints of footprints, only to have them swept away by the tide, it speaks to the beauty of release. It teaches us that nothing is fixed, and through this letting go, there is always space for renewal.

As I watched my children scoop and mould it, laughing as their creations fell apart and began again, I thought about how sand also holds the wisdom of play. It asks us to embrace the joy of imperfection and the freedom in allowing things to be unformed, undone, and recreated.

Mother Earth speaks through sand, her voice soft yet powerful. It reminds us to expand our perspective, to see not just the grains beneath our feet but the vastness of all that connects us. Each grain is part of the whole, shaped by forces we often cannot see, much like ourselves.

In the presence of the beach and the wisdom of sand, I found not just grounding but an expansive sense of connection. It reminded me that, like sand, we too are part of something far greater, carried by the currents of life, shaping and being shaped, endlessly transforming.

Graceful Reminder
I am part of the whole, ever-changing and endlessly connected to the wisdom of the Earth.

Devotion in the Cosmos

Look to the stars.

Each star is a pulse in the vast cosmic web, a thread in the intricate fabric of existence that binds us all. Just as a single star burns brightly in the infinite sky, so too does your soul burn with purpose, your light an irreplaceable part of the whole.

You are never separate. You are connected to everything.

To the Earth beneath your feet, to the heavens above, to every heartbeat, and every whisper of wind.

The universe is not just a space in which you exist. It is the very energy that flows through you, guiding your steps, supporting your choices.

The stars are not above you, but with you, part of you, woven into the same cosmic dance.

Devotion is the sacred act of recognising this interconnectedness.

To be devoted is to be in constant reverence of the web that holds all things.

It is the soft surrender to the flow of life, knowing that each step you take, no matter how small, is a movement in harmony with the universe.

You are not alone in your devotion. Your soul is held by the stars, the Earth, and all the beings that share this sacred journey with you.

Every moment of devotion is a return to this knowing.

It is the choice to listen to the whispers of the stars, to trust that their light guides you, as they have guided countless souls before you.

A dance of love and trust. It is a remembrance that the stars are not far off, but within, illuminating your path as you continue to unfold.

Know that as you move through the world with a heart devoted to love, to truth, and to the greater whole, you are aligning yourself with the stars.

Their light lives within you, just as your light lives within them. The universe is a mirror, reflecting your devotion back to you in every sparkling star, every quiet moment of stillness, every breath you take.

The Magic of Devotion

Devotion is the thread that connects us to the magic of the universe. It grounds us in the present, helping us process emotions, embody our true selves, and transform in ways we never thought possible. Through devotion, we not only grow but expand into the fullest expression of who we are meant to be.

I've come to understand that when we are intentional about our devotion whether it's to ourselves, others, God, universe, or the infinite, we open the doors to breaking through limitations we once thought were unmovable. It's in those small, deliberate acts of love and care that we tap into our internal medicine, the wisdom that resides deep within us, just waiting to be acknowledged.

As I sit under the Jacaranda tree in my backyard, the branches heavy with blooms, I feel the magic of devotion in its simplest form. I remember a moment not long ago when I was struggling to find clarity, feeling caught between old ways of thinking and the call of something new. I sat beneath this same tree, its soft purple petals carpeting the earth around me, and I allowed myself to simply *be*. No agenda, no expectations, just my breath and the rhythm of the world around me. In that stillness, I felt an overwhelming sense of connection, not just to the tree, but to the Earth, to the sky, to everything.

In that stillness, I realised how devotion works like this, a consistent force that helps us align our inner world with the outer world. When we devote ourselves to our growth, to our healing, to showing up as our true selves, we begin to dissolve the stuckness that holds us back. Each moment of devotion attunes our frequency, shifting the vibration of our being so we can expand beyond what we once believed possible. It is through this energetic devotion that transformation becomes not just an act but a state of resonance with the divine. It is through devotion that we can transition from one state of being to another, shedding old patterns, and stepping into what truly matters. We unlock our capacity to love deeper, to feel safe in the flow of life, and to embrace the magic that's always there, waiting to be rediscovered.

Devotion invites us to let go of control and trust in the unfolding. It's not about achieving perfection but about showing up, time and time again, with an open heart and a willingness to expand. It's the power that helps us rise, guides us through change, and carries us toward the life we're meant to live.

You'll often find me sitting under my Jacaranda tree when I'm in my backyard. In those moments, I'm reminded that devotion is a way of being. And in that stillness, I remember, this is where the magic begins.

Embodied Insight
What does devotion mean to you in your everyday life?
Explore how you show up for what matters most—whether it's to yourself, others, Mother Earth, or the Infinite. How do you express your devotion through small actions or choices that align with your values and purpose?

PART TEN

Integration

The Path You Walked

Throughout this book, you have been invited to meet yourself with grace. Not just in thought, but in feeling, sensation, and presence.

You have explored the language of your body, learning to attune to the messages of your nervous system. You have practised cultivating safety within, trusting your Intuitive Intelligence®, and softening into your capacity to feel, love, and heal. You have met the parts of you that live beneath the surface. Your emotions, fears, and tender truths. You have touched shame, not to dwell in it, but to shed the weight of it. You have practised radical acceptance, again and again. Devotion remains, holding space for each step you take.

And now, here you are. Integrating the journey.

Presence, humility, and loving action have guided your path. They aren't steps, but a way of being, a return to self.

Every time you stayed rather than abandoned: *presence.*
Every time you softened into discomfort: *humility.*
Every time you reached for gentleness, especially when hard: *loving action.*

These moments create lasting change. They rewire your brain and nervous system.

Imagine your nervous system as a field of paths. The old ones, self-doubt, shame, perfectionism, are well worn. But with each moment of grace, you walk a new path. At first unfamiliar, but over time, familiar, safer, and stronger. Your body remembers, your nervous system begins to trust, and grace becomes lived.

The more you choose compassion, the further the old patterns fade. You are no longer who you were at the beginning, nor were you ever meant to stay there. You are remembering, rooting yourself into a new way of being. This is the work, this is the grace, and this is you, fully embodied.

Embodied Insight
*What path are you walking now? How do presence, humility, and
loving action want to move through you next?*

Trusting of Grace

Integration is a continuation of trust, a letting grace flow through your life in ways both quiet and profound. Grace is not abstract. It is the steady presence that has always been here, guiding you as you move forward. I learnt this when I stepped away from frontline policing after years of carrying the weight of trauma, both my own and others. Leaving that role was not easy. It felt like letting go of certainty and stepping into the unknown. But I knew it was time. I had to trust that stepping away would not mean losing myself but finding myself.

I did not have a roadmap. I doubted, I questioned, I missed the clarity of a defined role. Yet each time I softened into trust, grace revealed itself. The resilience, empathy, and capacity to sit with discomfort that I had cultivated became the very gifts I now carry into my work as a somatic practitioner and intuitive somatic mentor. Trusting grace does not mean doing nothing. It means releasing the need to force and control. It is choosing to believe that every step matters, even when you cannot see how it all fits together.

Embodied Insight
*Where in your life are you holding onto control, and how might you
soften into trust to let grace guide you?*

Lightness of Love

I had travelled all the way to India, seeking something deeper than just the physical experience of being in a new place. I was in Auroville, and the Matrimandir, the golden sphere that stood at its very heart, called me to its sacred space. From the moment I set my eyes on it, I could feel that something profound was about to unfold, something beyond my understanding at the time, yet unmistakably powerful.

I walked toward the Matrimandir, each step carrying me closer to a transformation I couldn't yet comprehend. As I entered the golden sphere, the air itself seemed to shift. There was a palpable sense of reverence, as if the very building was breathing with me, guiding me toward stillness. The sun outside was bright, but as I stepped inside, the space felt heavy with quiet anticipation. It was almost as though the whole world had been paused, and only the present existed.

I made my way to the meditation room, my heart beating faster, sensing that something significant was about to happen. In this room, the darkness enveloped me, broken only by a single beam of light descending from the towering ceiling, casting a soft glow upon a handmade crystal at the base. The crystal, an offering of beauty and purity, seemed to call me in, inviting me to sit with it, to sit with *myself*.

As I settled into the room's stillness, I closed my eyes, feeling the surrounding air. I could hear my breath, steady and rhythmic with each inhale and exhale syncing with my body in a gentle, familiar dance. The energy around me felt like it was both ancient and new, and I could sense the space was holding me, offering me the opportunity to truly *be*.

Then, without warning, something shifted. It wasn't sudden or jarring, but gentle, a slow unravelling, as though the universe had taken a deep breath alongside me. I felt an incredible expansion within my chest, a lightness that began at the core of my being and radiated outward through every limb, every cell, every part of me. My body, once dense with the weight of years, suddenly felt weightless and free. It was as though I was being held by an invisible force which carried me beyond time and space.

And then, in the quiet of the darkness, I experienced a profound moment of self-love. It wasn't an intellectual understanding of love, but a *feeling*—pure and undeniable. I felt love for myself, for who I was, and for all the moments that had led me to that place. It was not the love we so often seek from others, but the deepest kind of love, one that flows from within, unconditional and complete.

It was then that I gave myself permission to *receive* my love. And with that permission, tears began to stream down my face. Not tears of sorrow or loss, but tears of profound acceptance and grace. The weight of all the years I had carried, the expectations, the struggles, the self-doubt. All of it melted away as I embraced this raw, vulnerable truth.

I am worthy of my love. I am enough.

As I sat there, tears silently flowing, I knew I was being true to myself in a way I had never allowed before. There, in the stillness of the Matrimandir, I experienced what it truly meant to honour my heart. I had created space for my love to fill me, heal me, and expand me.

The light from the crystal seemed to glow even brighter, as if echoing the light that had expanded within me. I felt a deep, sacred connection to myself, to all beings, and to the universe. The love I felt in that room was not separate from the world, it was the very fabric of the world itself, and I was part of it. I was the love, and the love was me.

I left that room forever changed, carrying the memory of that deep, transformative experience with me. But more than that, I carried the lesson that the love we seek is already within us, and it is only in stillness, in presence, in the willingness to receive it, that we can experience its true power.

The Matrimandir, in all its beauty and sacredness, had offered me something much deeper than I could have ever expected. It had shown me the path to my heart, a path that would continue to unfold long after I left that space.

That moment in the Matrimandir was a turning point. It was the moment I gave myself permission to *receive* my love, to let go of the self-imposed barriers, and to expand into the fullness of who I was meant to be. And in that expansion, I became more of myself than I had ever known before.

Graceful Reminder
True transformation begins when we give ourselves permission to receive our own love. In the stillness of presence, we discover that the love we seek is already within us, waiting to expand and fill every corner of our being.

Living Embodied Grace

As we reach the final steps of this journey, we do not end, we begin again, but differently. With more awareness. With a softened heart. With grace now woven through your being.

Integration is not about arriving somewhere new. It is how what you have touched, uncovered, and remembered begins to move through your life in the way you breathe, relate, choose, and live.

Grace is found in the breath before responding, in choosing self-kindness over self-criticism, in the willingness to let yourself be seen, even by yourself. It whispers in the discomfort of uncertainty, reminding you that you are exactly where you need to be. It does not demand perfection or constant attention. Instead, it invites you to return again and again, without pressure, without shame, simply with presence. Sometimes grace manifests in stillness, other times in the courage to ask for help. Sometimes it appears messy, wobbly, or unsure, and yet it is still grace.

You do not need to try harder to integrate what you have learned. Integration asks only that you return to your breath, your body, and to your truth.

This is how you embody grace.
This is how the extraordinary becomes ordinary.
This is how the truths you have remembered come alive in the everyday.

There is no finish line, only unfolding, only the continual expansion of yourself. Let grace walk with you, soft, steady, and true. You are ready, and grace has always been within you.

Graceful Reminder

Integration with grace is an intimate unfolding, a return to yourself that expands with each breath.

No More Waiting

For so long, I lived in the *almost*.
Almost ready.
Almost worthy.
Almost brave enough to take up space.

Waiting to wear certain clothes once I lost some weight.
Waiting to apply for positions once I felt more qualified.
Waiting to rest once everything on my to-do list was done.
Waiting to speak up once I felt more confident.
Waiting to invest in myself once I felt 'worthy' of it.
Waiting to pursue my dreams once life felt more stable.
Waiting to set boundaries once I felt stronger.
Waiting to prioritise my joy once everyone else was taken care of.
Waiting to be seen once I felt less afraid.

But life isn't lived in waiting rooms.
I won't wait anymore, hoping for space to open.
I won't wait to take up space.
I will claim it.

Because my voice matters. My presence matters.
I matter.

No more shrinking. No more second-guessing. No more waiting for someone else to make room.
We are here. We belong. And we are worthy of taking up every inch of space our soul desires.

PART ELEVEN

The Ongoing Journey

Reclaiming Your Truth

The experiences, graceful reminders, embodied insights, and practices shared throughout this book have guided me on this path, and they are here to support you in honouring your healing journey and reclaiming aspects of yourself that may have been forgotten. This journey invites you to embrace your inherent worthiness and reminds you that you are whole just as you are. It encourages you to listen to the wisdom within your body and allow it to lead you back to a place of full humanity.

Through this path, we discover that true grace is not an external goal but a state of being waiting to be uncovered. It is an intuitive knowing that you are enough. As you continue to embody this grace, may you walk with self-compassion and trust that each moment brings you closer to your radiant and empowered self.

As we approach the end of this book, remember that this practice is ongoing. It honours your depth and your healing. The journey is uniquely personal and asks for patience, courage, and the willingness to meet yourself where you are. This is especially important during challenging times. The more you practise, the stronger your foundation becomes, supporting you through life's ups and downs.

Grace lives within you. It is reflected in the way you meet yourself—whether in moments of joy or in times of pain. Approaching yourself with this grace reminds you of your inherent worth and reassures you that you are enough.

As you move forward, remember that this practice is always within reach. By living with embodied grace, you make a commitment to yourself, a commitment to self-compassion, authenticity, and a deep sense of inner trust. May it guide you as you grow and expand into the fullness of who you are.

Graceful Reminder

You don't have to do more or be more worthy of grace. You already are.

You Are Enough

You are enough,
Always enough,
Perfect in your imperfection,
Sacred in your being,
Breathe,
Expand,
Embody,
And know that you are divine.

Warrior of Grace

Growing up, I was often told that I was 'too sensitive' or that I cared 'too much.' I remember sharing with others as a teenager that I wanted to become a police officer, and many of them laughed. They told me I couldn't handle it, that my sensitivity would make me weak. Even my mother, though I knew it came from a place of love, feared that my caring nature would leave me vulnerable in a world that often demanded strength in ways that she felt were foreign to me. She was worried my heart would be my downfall.

But I knew, deep down, I was more than just someone who felt deeply. I was a warrior.

I was a warrior when my father passed away when I was just twelve from suicide. I was a warrior in every moment I stood strong for my family, doing everything I could to support my siblings and mum. I was a warrior when I refused to follow the crowd and let others define who I should be.

Despite all the voices telling me I was too sensitive, I knew that my heart would make me a great police officer. My ability to care, truly care, was not a weakness. It was my strength. It was what would allow me to understand people on a deep level, to support them when they needed it most. So, I joined the police academy, and I did it with conviction. I embraced my empathy, my compassion, and my capacity to feel deeply. I knew these qualities would guide me as I took on the challenging work of being a detective. I became a warrior in the darkest moments of people's lives, offering a compassionate presence in situations that demanded both strength and deep care. My 'too much' became my greatest gift. I recognised my sensitivity for what it truly was—not a flaw, but a superpower.

It was this same caring nature that led me to the work I do now, helping others on their healing journey. Becoming a somatic practitioner and intuitive somatic mentor wasn't a random path. It was the next chapter of my warrior journey. My ability to feel, to sense, and to be present with others' pain became the foundation of my ability to guide others in their own healing.

In 2021, after completing an intense year of study with Dr. Ricci-Jane Adams at the Institute for Intuitive Intelligence, we gathered for our final online circle. Each of us received a channelled message from Dr Ricci-Jane Adams. When she reached me, within her message she called me a "Warrior of Grace."

The moment she spoke those words, I felt it deeply within my bones, my heart, my soul. It was like a spark ignited within me, an activation of something ancient and deeply rooted. I felt the presence of the warriors of grace who came before me—my ancestors, my lineage, standing with me, acknowledging me, and accepting me. I felt their strength, their courage, and their grace flow through me. Their energy surrounded me, filling me with a sense of belonging and knowing that this path, this journey of being a Warrior of Grace, was not just mine but a continuation of a legacy.

That's when I saw myself fully. I was not only a warrior. I was a Warrior of Grace, just as those before me had been. A warrior who could move through the world with love, and it was the very thing that connected me to a lineage of strength, compassion, and wisdom.

Now, as I walk this new path of supporting others as they heal and expand, I know that my journey is not just about finding strength, it's about embracing the grace that comes from fully accepting who I am. It's about turning every piece of me into a gift, no matter how others may have seen it before.

Graceful Reminder

When we step into the fullness of who we are, we stand not alone, but with a lineage of warriors of grace who believed in us before we ever did.

Lineage of Light

WOMEN THROUGH THE AGES HAVE BEEN WARRIORS. NOT IN BATTLE,
BUT IN SPIRIT, IN LOVE, IN TRUTH.

WARRIORS OF GRACE.

THEIR STRENGTH WAS NOT FORGED IN FORCE BUT IN THE QUIET
RESILIENCE OF THE HEART, THE SURRENDER OF TRUST IN THEIR OWN
WISDOM, AND THE SACRED KNOWING THAT GRACE IS NOT WEAKNESS
BUT POWER IN ITS PUREST FORM.

THEY HAVE WALKED BEFORE YOU, CLEARING PATHS UNSEEN,
WHISPERING COURAGE INTO THE WINDS THAT NOW REACH YOUR SOUL.
THEIR FOOTSTEPS ECHO IN YOUR BEING, REMINDING YOU THAT YOU,
TOO, CARRY THIS LINEAGE OF LIGHT.

YOU ARE A WARRIOR OF GRACE.

YOUR BATTLE IS NOT AGAINST THE WORLD BUT FOR THE FULLNESS
OF YOUR OWN BECOMING. YOU WIELD COMPASSION AS YOUR SWORD,
INTUITION AS YOUR GUIDE, AND THE STEADY PULSE OF YOUR OWN
HEARTBEAT AS A DRUM CALLING YOU HOME. THE WAY YOU RISE, THE
WAY YOU SOFTEN, THE WAY YOU TRUST THE WISDOM THAT STIRS
WITHIN YOU. THIS IS YOUR POWER.

DO YOU FEEL THEM WITH YOU? THE WOMEN WHO HAVE COME BEFORE?

THEY WALK BESIDE YOU, THEIR PRESENCE WOVEN INTO YOUR BONES, THEIR
VOICES HUMMING IN YOUR BREATH. THEY REMIND YOU THAT GRACE IS
NOT PASSIVE. IT IS THE FORCE THAT BENDS BUT NEVER BREAKS, THE LIGHT

THAT DOES NOT FLICKER IN THE WIND, THE KNOWING THAT YOU ARE HELD, ALWAYS.

TAKE A MOMENT. CLOSE YOUR EYES. FEEL THE LINEAGE OF GRACE COURSING THROUGH YOU. HOW DOES YOUR LIGHT EXPRESS ITSELF? IN WHAT WAYS DO YOU EMBODY THE WARRIOR OF GRACE IN YOUR OWN LIFE?

THIS IS YOUR TIME. THIS IS YOUR PATH. AND YOU DO NOT WALK IT ALONE.

The Hands That Hold You

Remember that moment? The moment you knew change was calling. Maybe it was a whisper, a nudge, or a deep knowing within your bones that something needed to shift.

As I wrote this book, I thought back to a massage I had received, surrendering to the hands that guided me through release. The ache in my neck, the tightness in my shoulders, the tension gripping my hips. These were not just physical burdens. They were echoes of holding too much for too long.

Embodied Grace reminded me of that massage. You know you need it, you know it will shift something within you. You lie on the table, the warmth of oil meeting your skin, the pressure of hands, stones, or even elbows pressing into the places that hold resistance. At first, it feels good, comforting, soothing. Then comes the deep work. The knots, the stuck places, the wounds beneath the surface. The body's silent stories.

You stay because you trust. Because your nervous system has learnt to hold you in safety, to expand its capacity for sensation, for discomfort, for release. Each breath becomes an invitation, a softening into grace. The hands of the masseuse move with intention, pressing into the places where pain resides, unravelling the tension that has shaped you.

There are moments of relief, discomfort, and realisation. Just like the journey of self-compassion, there is no rushing this process. You breathe through the sensations, welcoming the release of not only physical stiffness but also the burdens of fear, shame, and old stories long held.

And this is where self-compassion meets you, right at the edge of discomfort, in the tender places that ache for gentleness. It is in the breath you offer yourself when the pressure deepens, in the kindness that whispers, *"Stay, soften, you are safe here."* Self-compassion reminds us that we are not something to be fixed but something to be held with care. It is the presence that allows us to experience both the tension and the release, the pain and the healing, without judgement.

This is initiation. Saying yes to the work, to the unfolding.

This is awakening to your body's language, learning to listen, to trust what it's speaking through sensation and silence.

This is cultivating safety within, remaining present even when it feels intense.

This is the divine whisper of your intuitive wisdom, knowing when to surrender.

This is expanding your capacity for love, towards yourself, towards the body that has carried so much.

This is going beneath the surface, meeting emotions you didn't realise were stored in your very tissue.

This is shedding the burden of shame, letting go, breath by breath.

This is radical self-acceptance, choosing to stay with yourself, no matter what arises.

This is devotion, returning to the practice of care, again and again.

This is integration, stepping off the table, lighter, freer, and more connected to yourself.

Your breath becomes your devotion. Your body, a temple of grace. You leave, not just with loosened muscles but with a deepened relationship to yourself.

This is the journey. This is Embodied Grace.

And now, as you reach the final pages of this book, I invite you to take a moment to pause. How do you feel? What subtle shifts are present within your body, heart, and mind? Notice the space you have created within yourself.

How can you extend self-compassion beyond this moment?

What grace will you carry forward? What will you leave behind?

Breathe it in. Honour it. Trust it.

You are here. You are whole. You are grace embodied.

Embodied Insight
How can you extend self-compassion beyond this moment?
What grace will you carry forward? What will you leave behind?

Coming Home To Yourself

Nurturing your nervous system and strengthening your intuitive wisdom to embody grace is a journey of profound transformation, one that asks for patience, faith, and a deep commitment to yourself. It's natural to want to rush past this part, to long for quick fixes, but true healing doesn't work that way.

This path is a slow burn that strengthens your foundation for lasting change. It's in this sacred stretch that your nervous system learns how to hold the fullness of life with resilience and ease. It's where the cycles of old wounds lose their grip, and the loops that once kept you stuck begin to close.

This work is not something you simply do. It's an embodied practice, a way of being that invites you to connect deeply with yourself. Through intuitive somatic work, you don't just heal, you transform. It's about coming home to your body, to the wisdom within, and allowing grace to flow through every fibre of your being.

When you show up for this work, you're not just nurturing your nervous system, you're creating a ripple of grace that flows into every corner of your life. This is how you bring forth self-compassion. This is how you embody grace.

It's in the gentle moments of showing up for yourself, even when it's hard. It's in the courage to face the layers of your being with love, to honour your story while releasing the parts that no longer serve you. It's in the quiet yet profound decision to choose healing, growth, and transformation—one breath, one step, one moment at a time.

This is your journey to wholeness.
This is your return to radiance.

This is the gift you give yourself.
A life lived in harmony with your body, your heart, and your soul.

You are not alone in this work. With every step you take, you honour the unshakable truth that you are deserving of compassion, healing, and grace. The journey may be slow, but it is sacred. The transformation may take time, but it is timeless.

And as you continue, may you always remember: the wisdom is within you, the grace is already yours, and the power to heal has always been in your hands.

Here's to your journey, may it lead you home.

Graceful Reminder
Each step toward healing is an act of devotion to yourself. Walk with love, and grace will meet you there.

Everyday Moments

Imagine a world where grace is the lens through which you view every experience. A world where you respond to challenges with love instead of judgement, where acceptance flows freely through your words and actions, and where connection becomes the foundation of your relationships. In a world that often feels chaotic, what if you could create this space of grace, both within yourself and in the way you relate to others?

Grace is not just a passive, abstract concept. It is an active force that we can embody every single day. It is the embodiment of presence, where we show up fully in the moment, with our hearts open and our attention anchored in the now. It is the embodiment of humility, where we recognise our shared humanity and the strength in vulnerability. And it is the embodiment of loving action, where we translate our inner grace into tangible acts of kindness, compassion, and understanding.

Presence + Humility + Loving Action = Embodied Grace

Grace invites us to cultivate love in moments of difficulty, to show up for ourselves and others with compassion, and to soften our hearts, even when the world around us feels overwhelming. It's in our imperfections that grace is most powerful. It's in those moments where we are able to forgive ourselves and others that grace flows most freely.

As we embody grace, we are called to be present in every moment, grounded, mindful, and aware. We give ourselves permission to show up fully in the world as we are, embracing the whole of who we are, including our imperfections, struggles, joys, and triumphs. This presence invites us to pause, listen, and respond from a place of compassion rather than reaction.

Grace is also a practice of humility. Recognising that we are not perfect but inherently worthy of love and kindness just as we are. This humility invites us to fully accept our humanity, gently releasing the grip of shame and the need for perfection. As we cultivate this compassionate acceptance within ourselves, we create an inner safety that naturally flows outward, allowing us to hold space for others with greater ease and presence. It is in embracing our own humanness that true healing and authentic connection arise.

And grace manifests through loving action. When we honour the love we cultivate within by expressing it through how we live, how we care for ourselves, and how we show up in the world. Loving action is about translating our inner state of grace into real, meaningful gestures of kindness, understanding, and support to ourselves. It's the ability to show up for ourselves with a heart full of compassion, embracing our imperfections and needs, and gently holding ourselves through every moment of struggle and growth.

When we embody grace through presence, humility, and loving action, we don't just create change in our own lives, we create a ripple effect that extends outward. Our grace becomes a source of healing for others, an invitation for them to step into their own truth and grace. It inspires those around us to do the same, nurturing a world that is kinder, more understanding, and deeply connected.

This is the beauty of grace. Its power to heal, uplift, and guide us back to one another. As we embody grace, we create a space for growth, for healing, for expansion, and for transformation. We become the source of love and compassion in a world that so desperately needs it. By cultivating presence, humility, and loving action, we come home to ourselves and to each other, one small, powerful act of grace at a time.

Grace is not for the perfect moments. It is born in the messy, imperfect, and unpredictable moments of life. And it is in these moments that we discover our true strength, beauty, and power. The power to heal, grow and reconnect with the essence of who we are and who we can be together.

As we embody grace, we lead by example. We heal ourselves, and in doing so, we help heal the world. One act of presence, one act of humility, and one act of loving action at a time.

Embodied Grace is here, and it is yours to live. This is your journey home.

Grace in Your Bones

MAY YOU KNOW THAT GRACE IS NOT SOMETHING YOU REACH FOR.
IT RISES FROM WITHIN YOU, THE WAY TRUTH DOES WHEN YOU STOP TRYING
TO BE ANYTHING OTHER THAN YOURSELF.

MAY IT FIND YOU IN THE PAUSES OF YOUR DAY,
IN A SIMPLE BREATH,
IN THE MOMENTS YOU CHOOSE TO TRUST YOURSELF EVEN WHEN THINGS
FEEL A LITTLE SHAKY.
YOUR BODY KNOWS THE WAY.
YOUR HEART HAS ALWAYS HELD THE MAP.

MAY IT SIT WITH YOU IN THE PLACES THAT ACHE,
THE TENDER PARTS YOU HAVE LEARNED TO TUCK AWAY.
NOTHING IN YOU IS TOO BROKEN OR TOO SLOW.
YOUR UNFOLDING HAS ITS OWN RHYTHM, AND GRACE MEETS YOU THERE,
SOFT, PATIENT, WITHOUT PRESSURE.

MAY IT HOLD YOU AS YOU GROW BEYOND WHAT YOU ONCE IMAGINED,
AS YOU STRETCH INTO YOUR FULLNESS,
INTO YOUR WISDOM,
INTO THAT WILD AND LUMINOUS SELF YOU KEEP MEETING IN PIECES.

NOT TO FIX YOU.
NOT TO TIDY YOU UP.
BUT TO WITNESS YOUR BECOMING,
TO HONOUR YOUR COURAGE,
TO AFFIRM THAT WHOLENESS HAS ALWAYS LIVED INSIDE YOU.

STACEY WEBB

And as you close these pages and step back into your life, let this
be with you:
Grace is not a finish line.
It is a presence.
A pulse within you.
A soft place in your body that knows the way home.

Walk on with grace in your bones and trust in your heart.

Bibliography

Adams, R.-J. (2022). *Subconscious fear release: Advanced practice* [Guided meditation]. Insight Timer. https://insighttimer.com/riccijane/guided-meditations/subconscious-fear-release-advanced-meditation [accessed 06 April 2025]

Atkinson, J. (2002). *Trauma trails, recreating song lines: The transgenerational effects of trauma in Indigenous Australia.* Spinifex Press.

Brach, T. (2003). *Radical acceptance: Embracing your life with the heart of a Buddha.* Bantam Books.

Brown, B. (2012). *Daring greatly: How the courage to be vulnerable transforms the way we live, love, parent, and lead.* Gotham Books.

Chödrön, P. (2002). *When things fall apart: Heart advice for difficult times.* Shambhala.

Dalai Lama XIV, & Cutler, H. C. (1998). *The art of happiness.* Riverhead Books.

Dana, D. (2023). *Anchored: How to befriend your nervous system using polyvagal theory.* Sounds True.

Dana, D. (2018). *Polyvagal exercises for safety and connection: 50 client-centred practices.* Norton & Company.

Dana, D. (2020). *The polyvagal theory in therapy: Engaging the rhythm of regulation.* W. W. Norton & Company.

Easwaran, E. (2007). *The Bhagavad Gita.* Nilgiri Press.

Ferguson, A. (2023). *The vagus nerve reset: Train your body to heal stress, trauma, and anxiety*. Ebury Publishing.

Hooks, B. (2000). *All about love: New visions*. William Morrow.

Kuburic, S. (2023). *It's on me: Accept hard truths, discover your self, and change your life*. Penguin Life.

McGrath, A. (2016). *Christian theology: An introduction* (6th ed.). Wiley-Blackwell.

Merton, T. (1961). *New seeds of contemplation*. New Directions Publishing.

Merton, T. (1966). *Conjectures of a guilty bystander*. Doubleday.

Moltmann, J. (1993). *Theology of hope*. SCM Press.

Myss, C. (2023). *A time for grace: Sacred guidance for everyday life*. Hay House.

Nakata, M. (2007). *Disciplining the savages, savaging the disciplines*. Aboriginal Studies Press.

Neff, K. (2011). *Self-compassion: The proven power of being kind to yourself*. William Morrow.

O'Donohue, J. (1997). *Anam cara: A book of Celtic wisdom*. HarperCollins.

Porges, S. W. (2011). *The polyvagal theory: Neurophysiological foundations of emotions, attachment, communication, and self-regulation*. W. W. Norton & Company.

Porges, S. W. (2022). *The Polyvagal Theory: Our Polyvagal World* [Video]. Polyvagal Institute. [accessed 25th May 2025]

Radhakrishnan, S. (1927). *The Hindu view of life*. Harper & Brothers.

Rose, D. B. (1992). *Dingo makes us human: Life and land in an Australian Aboriginal culture*. Cambridge University Press.

Schwartz, R. C. (1995). *Internal family systems therapy*. Guilford Press.

Thich Nhat Hanh. (1998). *The heart of the Buddha's teaching*. Parallax Press.

References

1. Dana, D. (2020). *The polyvagal theory in therapy: Engaging the rhythm of regulation*. W. W. Norton & Company.

2. Schwartz, R. C. (1997). *Internal family systems therapy*. Guilford Press. p.30-42

3. Porges SW. Orienting in a defensive world: mammalian modifications of our evolutionary heritage. A Polyvagal Theory. *Psychophysiology*. 1995;32(4):301-318. doi:10.1111/j.1469-8986.1995.tb01213.x [accessed 17 January 2025]

4. Dana, D. (2020). *The polyvagal theory in therapy: Engaging the rhythm of regulation*. W. W. Norton & Company.

5. Schwartz, R. C. (1997). *Internal family systems therapy*. Guilford Press. p.30-42

6. Adams, R.-J. (2022). *Superconscious intuition: Intuition beyond the trinkets and superstitions of the new age*. Institute for Intuitive Intelligence. p13

7. Adams, R.-J. (2019). *Spiritually Fierce: Are you ready to surrender to your unlimited self?* Institute for Intuitive Intelligence. p19

8. McCraty, R. (2015). *Science of the heart: Exploring the role of the heart in human performance* (Vol. 2). HeartMath Institute. https://www.heartmath.org p24-28

9. ScienceDirect Topics. (n.d.). *Nonverbal Behavior*. In *ScienceDirect*. https://www.sciencedirect.com/topics/neuroscience/nonverbal-behavi

or/ [accessed 20th January 2025]

10. McCraty, R. (2015). *Science of the heart: Exploring the role of the heart in human performance* (Vol. 2). HeartMath Institute. https://www.heartmath.org p36-44

11. Armour, J. A. (2007). The little brain on the heart. *Cleveland Clinic Journal of Medicine,* S48–S53.

12. McCraty, R. (2015). *Science of the heart: Exploring the role of the heart in human performance* (Vol. 2). HeartMath Institute. https://www.heartmath.org p3-7

13. McCraty, R. (2015). *Science of the heart: Exploring the role of the heart in human performance* (Vol. 2). HeartMath Institute. https://www.heartmath.org p24-28

14. Adams, R.-J. (2022). *Superconscious Intuition: Intuition beyond the trinkets and superstitions of the new age.* Institute for Intuitive Intelligence. p126

15. Williamson, M. (1996). *A return to love.* HarperCollins. p149

16. Swart, T. (2019). *The source: Open your mind, change your life.* Hachette Australia. p124

17. Simeona, M. N. (1980s). Modern Hoʻoponopono teachings. Foundation of I, Inc. Freedom of the Cosmos. Adapted and later popularised by Dr. Ihaleakala Hew Len.

Resources

Within these pages, you'll find echoes of many teachers, mentors, and sacred lineages who have shaped and nurtured this journey. To honour their gifts and support your own exploration, this section offers a collection of resources that have deeply influenced this work and can serve as companions on your path.

Andee Love: https://andeelove.com/
Dr Ricci-Jane Adams: https://www.riccijaneadams.com/
Dr Stephen Porges: https://www.stephenporges.com/
HeartMath® Institute: https://www.heartmath.org/
Internal Family Systems: https://ifs-institute.com/
Institute for Intuitive Intelligence:
https://instituteforintuitiveintelligence.com/
Kristin Neff: https://self-compassion.org/
Polyvagal Institute: https://www.polyvagalinstitute.org/
School of Somatic Arts: https://theschoolofsomaticarts.com/
Somatic Experiencing: https://www.somaticexperiencing.com/
The Centre for Healing: https://www.thecentreforhealing.com/

Thank You

To every reader of this book, I offer my deepest gratitude. Thank you for taking this journey of Embodied Grace alongside me, for opening your heart, and for exploring the depths of self-compassion and inner wisdom.

Your willingness to engage with this work, to show up for yourself with kindness and curiosity, is a profound act of courage. It is my hope that the stories, practices, and insights shared here have offered you new ways to connect with yourself and navigate your life with more grace and compassion.

Thank you for trusting in the process, for embracing your own unique path, and for allowing me to be a part of it. Your journey matters, and it is through each step you take toward self-compassion that you contribute to a more loving, authentic, and empowered world.

So much love, Stacey

Letter of Gratitude

To my husband Grant, thank you for your continued support and for never flinching when I say, "I have an idea…" even if it's the tenth one this week. For walking beside me through every wild vision, offering your calm presence, practical wisdom, and wholehearted encouragement. I am so grateful for the co-creative life we share and the love that moves through all we do together.

To my children Vanessa, Rhiannon, Ashton, and Adeline, thank you for choosing me to be your mother. You remind me daily of what matters most. You are my greatest teachers, my heart made visible.

To my book coach Vanessa Barrington and editor Dannielle Line, thank you for your guidance, insight, and care through each stage of this process. Your expertise and thoughtful contributions helped me bring clarity and coherence to my words, allowing Embodied Grace to emerge in its truest form.

To Ilonka Lucas, the first person I shared Embodied Grace with in India, and who held the vision with me. Your support, insight and deep belief carried me through every stage of bringing this book to life.

To Dr Ricci-Jane Adams, thank you for your fierce love and luminous guidance as I moved through the many drafts of this book. Your mentorship is both fire and grace, and I am forever changed by it.

Thank you to Tosca Dee, Lisa Benson, Alison Haitana, and Sonee Singh for walking alongside me during the early shaping of this book. Your thoughtful reflections, honest feedback and generous hearts helped me bring greater clarity, depth and resonance to these pages.

To all of my clients, in every capacity, and to every person who has engaged with my work, thank you. It has been an honour and a privilege to witness your journeys, courage, and unfolding. The sacred spaces we have shared, your presence, and your transformation have deeply shaped this book. Embodied Grace carries your essence within its pages.

And thank you again to you, dear reader. I am deeply grateful that you have chosen to hold this book in your hands. Your openness and willingness to journey with these words mean more than I can express. It is an honour to share this space of healing and grace with you.

So much love, Stacey

Where to Find Me

Before you close this book, I want to remind you that I'm here as someone who genuinely wants to support you on your healing journey. If you feel called to connect, whether to explore working together or to simply reach out, I would love to hear from you. You can find me through my website or on social media, where I share insights and tools to help you embrace self-compassion and Embodied Grace.

Website
https://www.staceywebb.com.au

facebook.com/StaceyWebbEFT

instagram.com/_staceywebb

amazon.com/author/staceywebb

goodreads.com/author/show/22384693.Stacey_Webb

tiktok.com/@_staceywebb

youtube.com/@Staceywebb

About the Author

Stacey Webb is an Intuitive Somatic Mentor, Somatic Practitioner, Warrior of Grace, and author devoted to guiding individuals on a graceful journey of self-compassion and intuitive intelligence. She creates transformative spaces that support personal growth and healing.

Her work is deeply shaped by her unique journey from serving as a detective in the police force to becoming a somatic practitioner. Witnessing the profound impact of trauma firsthand, Stacey recognised the need for holistic approaches to healing. Through her personal experience and professional training, she has developed a compassionate understanding of the body's natural capacity to heal and the powerful role of grace in this process.

Stacey helps clients expand their nervous system's capacity for safety, hold themselves with kindness, and trust their inner wisdom. She empowers them to release self-criticism, embody grace, and step into wholeness.

Based in Sydney, Australia, with her husband and four children, Stacey lives her journey of Embodied Grace each day, shaping how she moves through life and how she nurtures her family. She believes that cultivating self-compassion, safety, and inner wisdom helps her children grow into their authentic selves with confidence, curiosity and kindness.

Through her writing, workshops, and mentorships, Stacey's mission is to help people bring grace into their daily lives while building a deep sense of worthiness, connection, and trust in their own journey. *Embodied Grace* is an expression of that mission, a heartfelt invitation to rediscover your own power of self-compassion, inner wisdom, and embodied healing.

Also by Stacey Webb

Books

The Intuitive Detective

Foundations of Tapping: Inviting EFT and Other Tapping Practices Into Your Life

Foundations of Tapping: Companion Workbook

Cards

Embodied Grace: Trusting Yourself, Healing Deeply, Expanding Fully – Graceful Reminder Cards